SAGGISTICA 6

An Italian Writer's Journey through American Realities: Giose Rimanelli's English Novels

"The most tormented decade of America: the 60s"

Sheryl Lynn Postman

Bordighera Press

Library of Congress Control Number: 2011945039

The author and publisher warmly thank Alessandro Marrone for use of his painting
Paolo e Francesca.
www.alessandromarrone.it

© 2012, the Author

All rights reserved. Parts of this book may be reprinted only by written permission from the author/publisher, and may not be reproduced for publication in book, magazine, or electronic media of any kind, except in quotations for purposes of literary reviews by critics.

Printed in the United States.

Published by
BORDIGHERA PRESS
John D. Calandra Italian American Institute
Queens College
25 West 43rd Street
New York, NY 10025

SAGGISTICA 6
ISBN 978-1-59954-034-4

To my husband,
and to all who endured those "tormented" years, the 60s,
I dedicate this book.

Table of Contents

Preface (1)

Chapter 1: A Cracked Mirror, A Fragmented History And A Path That Always Comes Back to The Beginning: Giose Rimanelli's *Benedetta in Guysterland* (7)

Chapter 2: "She's Just a Devil Woman with Evil on Her Mind": Giose Rimanelli's *Accademia* (51)

Chapter 3: The Long and Winding Road in Giose Rimanelli's *The Three-Legged One* (98)

Index of Names (151)

About the Author (153)

Preface

Ten years ago I published a collection of nine essays, each on a different novel, of the Italian narratives of Giose Rimanelli. The book was entitled *Crossing the Acheron: A Study of Nine Novels by Giose Rimanelli* (Legas, 2000). At that time, I limited myself to a definitive number of narrations by the author. Through the years I have continued my research on Rimanelli's Italian works writing an additional three essays on his tales that he wrote in the United States and published in Italy within the recent past few years.

In all of the narrations which I discuss in *Crossing the Acheron*, a prominent theme emerges from the author's work: the abuse of political power within the governing bodies of the day. *Tiro al piccione* tells the story of a young boy fighting in the Italian Civil war on the wrong side; *Peccato originale* relates the story of social inequity, an inequality that demands the poor southern Italian to immigrate in search of a better life; *Una posizione sociale* handles the prewar period of the 1930s and compares the Fascist regime of Italy with the societal and political malaise of the southern United States, specifically New Orleans of the late 1800s; *Biglietto di terza* traces the immigrant experience, initiated in *Peccato originale*, to its fruition in the new land of Canada; *Il mestiere del furbo* recounts the stranglelike political and social grip of the publishing industry and the patron system on the young writer in Italy; *Tragica America* takes the reader on a journey through America during the turbulent 1960s and the period of assassinations, race riots, and antiwar protests; *Graffiti* depicts, in a totally negative fashion, the dominating male behavior toward the female by subjugating her to his will and insinuating the need to allow her to grow and blossom within a new society rather than chain her to a medieval-like past; and *Detroit Blues* portrays the social and racial disparity of the United States in the 1960s.

Rimanelli's American novels, written in the author's adopted language of English, like his Italian narratives, deal with the political and societal perversion of a specific time period in the United States: the presidential years of Richard Nixon, a period that ranges from 1968 (his election) to August 1974 (his official resignation) and the socio political corruption that became part of the American fabric of life for years to come. In his narrative, *Tragica America*, the author refers to the 60s as *il decennio piú tormentato della storia dopo l'Unificazione e il New Deal*; hence, the title of this study on the author's English language novels. The careful reader of this writer's opus will notice that Rimanelli creates perceptible parallels between this historic moment in American history and the Fascist years of Mussolini in the Italian peninsula.

Additionally, in order to set in relief the infernal like conditions that existed in his new country during this tumultuous decade, the author relies on his Italian medieval literary tradition and the masterpiece of Dante Alighieri, *La divina commedia*, filters throughout his entire work. The subtle manipulation of the great Florentine is not haphazard nor is it superficial in these works of Rimanelli. It is, rather, specific and deliberate in its intent. Dante's Orphic journey takes place, as we all know, during the political turmoil of his lifetime. Rimanelli, in an analogous manner, also has us traveling down a similar and even more winding pathway through the political and social malaise of an era in order to highlight the unacceptable societal and bureaucratic realities of the day that permeated all aspects of American life.

At the same time, Rimanelli, ever cognizant of his medieval literary tradition, also alludes, through the subtext and structure of his narrative, to another great Italian writer, Giovanni Boccaccio. Like Boccaccio who wrote during the Black Plague of Italy generating a juxtaposition of the brilliant, plush gardens of Florence by underscoring the human horrors of his era in order to show the social and political malady of his day, Rimanelli centers his literary universe on the American University system and its so-called sheltered ivory towers setting it up against the governmental and cultural realities of his period so as to show that nothing is left untouched from illegal behavior. Ironically, it is Boccaccio who changes the name of Dante's *magnum opus* from *Commedia* to *La divina commedia* and validates the assiduousness to these two classic authors as a font for this contemporary writer in his new espoused home.

Nixon's tenure as President defined five crucial and relevant years in the political, social and cultural history of the country. During his Administration, Vietnam protests were growing in strength and in numbers. He extended, although promising to leave Vietnam during his 1968 campaign, the war offensive by entering into neighboring Cambodia. Campus student strikes erupted throughout the country. The Kent State Massacre took place in Ohio killing four students and wounding nine.

Women, since the nineteenth Century (Seneca Falls Declaration of Sentiments [1848]) were asking for equality under the law. The Nineteenth Amendment, although granting women the right to vote, did not give them equality in the eyes of the law. In 1972 the Equal Rights Amendment was passed in the Senate but failed to be ratified by enough States to make it a law. Women, to this day in the twenty-first century have, unfortunately, not been given the total legal equality they sought, although they have accomplished huge gains in a culture that has negated their economic freedom.

A pivotal year in the history of the country would prove to be 1972. The Presidential elections take place in November and Nixon is reelected to a second term in office. But it will, moreover, evidence the downfall of this seasoned politician due to the break-in of the Democratic National Committee headquarters at the Watergate Office Complex during the National Convention. Watergate becomes part of the nation's cultural, social, political and linguistic reality.

It was during the Vietnam War, in 1969, that Rimanelli became a citizen of the United States. He has often explained that the main reason for his doing so was to allow himself the entitlement that comes with being a registered voter in a nation that sanctions and endorses taking a stand, critically, for or against the government. Rimanelli's cultural perception was in opposition to the war in Southeast Asia.

He had, as attested with his first published novel, *Tiro al piccione*, witnessed, firsthand the horrors of a civil war in his native country that devastated and extinguished his own childhood. The stench and revulsion of that horrific, historical period in time (1943-1945) remained with him throughout his life and is clearly perceived, by the reader, within the majority of his literary works. War, any hostility, mandated by the author's own personal, horrifying experience, created his resistance to any justification of its atrocities.

Rimanelli's becoming a national of the United States, at this particular moment in time, permitted him to cast a much more analytical eye to the changing socio political environment that was now penetrating the nation. He was, therefore, the proverbial guest who sees more in an hour than the host in a year.

Each of these events plays an important role in Rimanelli's trilogy. *Benedetta in Guysterland* brings forth the voice of the unheard, underage majority in the military engagement of Southeast Asia that the political administration refused to consider and, ultimately, brought an end to an unjust and unsanctified conflict. *Accademia*, the story of an academic couple, goes beyond the simple tale of a failed mar-

"Preface"

riage and enters into the corrupt politics of the day and the administrative machinations that have an impact in the ivory towered community by employing the negative attributes of the feminist movement as an allegory to the current day political decline of the nation. *The Three-legged One*, a continuation and more thorough version of the earlier *Accademia*, handles the political cover-up of the Watergate debacle by relating it to the contemporary marital life of a couple on the verge of a divorce in the American university system.

These are not easy novels for the inexperienced reader. They attest to the author's artistic experimentation with his new language while incorporating, simultaneously, elements of his classic European education. I have only indicated possible interpretations from signs I perceived within the text. There are many more.

I would like to point out that these narratives conclude at the end of the second week of August 1974. There will be many who may believe, due to my personal relationship with the author, that my presence is ubiquitous within the pages of these narratives. It is not. I did not meet Giose until the final week of August 1974 when I appeared, at his table by mistake, for registration at the University for my graduate studies in Spanish. We became friends later and, as many of you know, married several years later.

At the end of my study *Crossing the Acheron*, I acknowledged the encouragement of a few chosen escorts on my journey through Giose Rimanelli's Italian narratives. Those guides were the protagonists in each of the novels discussed. At this time, I would, also, like to recognize the assistance of a few more companions on this new voyage through the American Rimanelli, and specify the following characters: Clarence 'Benedetta' Ashfield, Simon Dona, and his wife, Lisa/Vera Jones.

Sheryl Lynn Postman

A Cracked Mirror, A Fragmented History And A Path That Always Comes Back to The Beginning:
Giose Rimanelli's *Benedetta in Guysterland*[1]

Giose Rimanelli's first novel written in the English language, *Benedetta in Guysterland*,[2] is not a simple or easy text for the novice. The author, already established as part of the world of Italian letters of the post civil war years in the peninsula, moves to the United States at the very start of the 1960s, a decade that he describes, in his Italian book *Tragica America,* as "il decennio più tormentato della storia dopo l'Unificazione e il New Deal."[3] Historically, these ten, pivotal years in the United States manifest the coming of age of a young nation. It is a period in which the country loses it innocence with the assassination of a president; the assassination of a potential future president; the assassination of a civil rights leader; the engagement in an unpopular war; the introduction of equality of the races and genders; and the entrance of the nation into a heightened state of fear due to a cold war between two nuclear super powers. Rimanelli, in addition, states in *Tragica America* that the America in which he has arrived is an epoch that manifests:

> Una rivoluzione di carattere politico, economico, sociale, intellettuale, artistico e nichilistico, dalle diramazioni più sottili e tentacolari, è in atto sia nella vita del sottosuolo che alla luce aperta, e in sé avvolge, tra-

---

[1] This essay originally appeared in *Forum Italicum* 41.1 (Spring 2007): 79-110 and is included herein with permission from the journal.
[2] Giose Rimanelli, *Benedetta in Guysterland* (Montreal: Guernica Press, 1993); all future page references come directly from this text and will appear in parentheses.
[3] Giose Rimanelli, *Tragica America* (Genova: Immordino editore, 1968) 7.

volge e rigenera vecchie istituzioni e coscienze, modi di vita, di pensare, di agire, di ribellarsi, e in pratica di essere. (*Tragica America*, 8)

The reader of *Benedetta in Guysterland* is immediately thrust into a rapidly moving and constantly changing vortex of this decisive and combative era in America, and it manifests, within this text, by the use of language, a linguistic process that in this novel, explores, evolves and expands with each passing chapter. Comparable to the numerous lights and projections that reflect from a prism and spread out rapidly and diversely on a large white screen, refashioning a multiplicity of images that may stand individually by themselves or combine into one huge surrealistic Picasso like image, the unsuspecting lector becomes a witness to a defining moment in America's new dantean-like reality. The author presents a world in which the existing actuality is one of darkness and despair. The collective life with all its ramifications, oddities and elaborateness play out and dominate the current time. To spotlight the discernment and loss of hope of the present era in his new social environment (a defining moment in the American culture of the present day that scarred and changed the American political landscape for years to come), Rimanelli interweaves, within the current text, parallel situations of terror and dread that hurled the Italian peninsula, thirty years earlier, into its monstrous infernal of the Civil War. The author, relying on his classic, Italian medieval literary tradition, juxtaposes this contemporary historical period with the horrific reality of the Fascist era that engulfed the Italian peninsula from 1922-1945. In so doing, Rimanelli is crystallizing the gulf that exists between two very different generations that manifested itself as the "generation gap," a socio-political dilemma that engrossed the entire nation and threatened a war-like confrontation between the groups: father and son; mother and daughter; old and new ways of lifestyles and its perspectives. The impetus for this constant battle stance between the two opposing social groups was a defining moment in American international policy: the Vietnam War. He then, carefully, juggles two different historic periods within two diverse universes at two extremely critical moments in their social and political developments. In so doing, the distinctions and barriers that separate these two realities erode away and coalesce into one, showing that they actually flow, similar to liquid, from one sphere of existence into the other.

In order for the author to generate the essential binary passageway to escort us along through the social and political infernal of the 1960s, he must set in relief two specific time periods of analogous consternation: the European power struggle of the pre and World War II years; and the 60s, a period in which all actions initiated and introduced into the American culture by earlier generations, is now being questioned by a newer coeval of participants, younger and unwilling to accept, blindly, the old ways forced upon them by their elders in the society of today.

The basic story of *Benedetta in Guysterland* is simple. Benedetta comes from New Wye, (Nabokov County) in Appalachia, USA. She is a student at Anabais College, an institution of higher education for women that caters to the wealthy and elite. She is the lover of a powerful underworld figure, Joe Adonis. Adonis is the son of the Italian Mafioso Joseph Adonis (Giuseppe Doto) exiled by the United States to Italy for having lied to the United States government about his place of origin and rejected by Italy for his illegal practices in the New World. His son, Joe, however, born in the Bronx, has been exiled from the States and sent to Italy by the crime families of New York. Fearing the return of the youthful Adonis, Santo "Zip the Thunder" Tristano, nemesis and one time godfather of Joe, holds Benedetta captive. There is an underworld war between competing families taking place in the New York metropolitan area. One family pertains to the older generation, the forced immigrants who left Italy during the Fascist era, and the other family consists of those younger members who were born in the United States and lack the horrific experience of their elders. It is, ultimately, a conflict between the old and new schools, of thought and action, and the manner in which they handle a crisis. Joe belongs to one family and Zip the Thunder to another. Eventually, Joe returns and is killed by Zip the Thunder's crew. Once dead, Benedetta is set free. As she prepares to leave, she realizes that she is pregnant with the child of Joe.

The linguistic game plan pattern established in the preamble to the text, *For-a-word*, resonates throughout, and proposes, the overwhelming importance of language: its role in the narration, and, simultaneously, the function of the originator of the words. More important, it traces, with very limited and concise terminology, the rhetorical engagement of an author within literature from the earliest of times to the present moment. It is through the use of his newly acquired language, and deep comprehension and passion for it, that the author, an émigré, shows the reader the dilemmas and quandaries of a particular historic moment in time, the 1960s, in his recently espoused land, the United States. In his opening section of the novel Rimanelli states:

> At one time in my life, as a master-builder-producer in another country I was sick with language and style. My body was covered with sentences, words, newspaper print. Then I took a shower. The tattoo's still showing, because I was not at all convinced that one can free himself at once of the inherited malaise Also because, following afro St. Augustine, I was constantly praying: "O G-d, send me purity and continence - but not yet." (28)

In these few epigrammatic statements, the writer suggests that the antiquated theories of Vladamir Propp are still present and prevalent in the contemporary literary world. Contemporaneously, his objective is to change the function of the author, as the creator of the text, allowing for the possibility of a new, energetic style of artistic expression in which language plays a more dominant role, and the word itself creates the narrative, free from any personal baggage that the author may possess.

Propp proposes, in his *Morphology of the Folktale,* that fairytales have restricted basic theses and that these elements are, for the most part, repetitive in all narrative forms. He submits that all stories are, basically, variants of a single tale. They are modeled on fixed structures and prefabricated elements all of which are placed in a number of combinations.[4] Rimanelli, by stating that he "took a shower" but that "the tattoo is still showing" is attempting to free himself of this confining literary dogma in which the words of the text render the persona of the writer and, without forgetting nor negating his literary roots, is entering into a new stage in his creative triumph that permits the reader a considerable amount of interplay. The author's *cleansing* of his formalistic language and the traditional literary structures of the 1950s and earlier, echoes the theories that Italo Calvino proposes, more than six years after the start of *Benedetta in Guysterland.*

Calvino asserts that in the present day, man looks at the world from various directions all at once. He is bombarded by a world that is made up of abstract, and not continuous, elements. It is the conquest of the combination of the total of these elements over all that is flux that generates the new image. This idea closely resembles what Benedetta writes as she composes her letter to Joe:

---

[4] Vladamir Propp, *Morphology of the Folktale,* translated by Laurence Scott (Austin and London: University of Texas Press, 1979) 21-24.

> These thoughts live in my mind as they appear on the paper, muddled and, as I know only too well, unorganized. I feel that if I organize them, they will seem like an essay to me and I would not be writing for myself if I spent time arranging ideas into neat little compartments. Do you understand me, Joe? While I am writing, I am far away; and when I come back, I have already left. I am now pounding on the typewriter, talking to myself and at the same time listening to Zip and the Band downstairs and yet drinking of you, Joe. (40)

Benedetta does not look at the world with one perspective; it is multiple and varied, like the pieces of a huge jigsaw puzzle. Joe, accordingly, may take the assorted tiles, put them together and refashion a new portrait. At the same time, multiple tiles create the possibility for numerous representations, each correct from the perspective of the narrative's new creator: the word as perceived by the reader.

In the past, the writer existed within the act of writing, now authors must tear down and reassemble the process of literary composition.[5] Calvino, speaking of the function of literature, states:

> Literature is a combinatorial game that pursues the possibilities implicit in its own material, independent of the personality of the poet, but that it is a game that at a certain point is invested with an unexpected meaning, a meaning that is not patent on the linguistic plane on which we were working but has slipped in from another level, activating something that on that second level is of great concern to the author or his society. (22)

Rimanelli's *Benedetta in Guysterland* takes the traditional European novel, a formula that commenced *in illo tempore* with the storyteller, and converts it into a new American paradigm by reformulat-

---

[5] Italo Calvino, "Cybernetics and Ghosts" in *The Uses of Literature*, translated by Patrick Creagh (San Diego, New York, London: Harcourt Brace Jovanovich, Publishers, 1982) 7-10.

ing and reconstructing the configuration and language of the tale. He removes the author from the narrative, for being superfluous, and the text is, therefore, controlled by the reader who is being guided through the narrative by the language from within. The fable has, therefore, been reinvented.[6]

At the same time, although the author is re-inventing the physical formation of the narrative, the tangible configuration of the tale is reminiscent of Boccaccio's *Decameron*. The initial chapter, *For-a-word*, sets the stage for the entire text. It is in this segment that Rimanelli notifies us of his game plan strategy and the role that language will play within the book. Contrary to his earlier novels, the author tells us that he will not be the manufacturer of this work, but just the conveyor of the words and that this action frees him from the bondage of the plot. Elements that appear within this initial chapter, ultimately, resurface within the volume, as in the case of Boccaccio's work. Additionally, within the twenty-eight chapters of Benedetta's tale, there are anecdotal digressions that deal with the book as a whole and that, at the same time, can stand independently from each other. As Boccaccio innovated the tale, presenting the archetypical storyline with its formalistic organization and language, Rimanelli's fable, on the other hand, inaugurates a new and exciting postmodern construction, a giant leap forward that conducts us into the future of literature, verifying his initial statement of being "an architect, a city planner..." (27).

Structurally, the narrative is presented in three parts with two distinct voices. The first and last part consists of one chapter each and is recounted by the author. The last chapter, the *Post-Word*, specifically deals with the anecdotal after effects of the main segment. The first chapter, *For-a-word*, deals with a brief literary history of

---

[6] For a similar reading, see Anthony Julian Tamburri, *A Semiotic of Ethnicity: In (Re)cognition of the Italian/American Writer* (Albany: SUNY 1998) 65.

this specific writer and his search for a new linguistic style that he pursues in the center. The middle division, twenty-eight chapters, forms the bulk of the narration, and is told, in the first person singular voice of Benedetta. She is typing her story while being held captive by Zip. Actual and fictitious people combine and interact within the dual universes of the past and present. Benedetta is held prisoner, for one week, of the opposing criminal family that migrated to the States at the birth of tyranny in the Old World. Her narrative, in addition, relates various episodes that go back in time and trace the early stages of Fascism in Italy. Time, however, is fragmentary and not chronological. It fluctuates between the present and the past and is shown, ingeniously in this narrative, kindling the literary idea of time, in that Benedetta is reading Proust.[7] Additionally, in the protagonist's opening moment of her letter to Joe Adonis, she states "Time lost its shoes. A year is four centuries." These words reverberate, simultaneously, those of the writer who in his *For-a-word* expounds:

> "You stupid. If we take eternity to mean not infinite temporal duration but timelessness, the eternal life belongs to those who live in the present." Thus, one day is enough if only the mind could be cauterized of all its secret calls. (29)

The extrapolating view of time, from the perspective of both the author and the protagonist, allows for the rapid shifting of historical instants between the universe that existed in Europe during the twenty years of the totalitarian dictatorship and the democratic

---

[7] "Looking back on something with different eyes is always startling. It is like looking into a kaleidoscope in which the glass chips are arranged very neatly in a regular, clear pattern. The next look into the kaleidoscope, perhaps months or years later reveals irregularities and the flaws in what then seemed like an ideal situation. In the reds and purples there are now blacks and slivers of shattered chips. I was reading Proust" (121).

American government that exists now during this pivotal period of social, political, cultural metamorphosis or that seems to be, during this decisive period, in a state of constant instability. Additionally, the view of time portrayed by the author and the protagonist license the intermingling of these two very diverse and culminating moments in the psyche of two disparate and yet, similar generations, thereby fostering the continuation of the dual environment established within the narrative.

The dimorphous universe through which the author guides the reader is presented with the appearance of characters who have experienced the two diverse worlds: the mafia-like older immigrants who, outlawed and persecuted during the Fascist era for their illegal acts, came to the United States and prospered, only to imitate the restrictive and odious policies of a government that mistreated them in their exiled homeland. The unifying element between the two divergent eras is the presence of the younger Joe Adonis, born in America but educated in Italy. Joe has a more liberal and open position to the American lifestyle. It contradicts sharply with the perspective of his father's generation, a group of immigrants that was forced into exile and, coincidentally, forced to follow the traditions of an earlier group that oppressed them.

In addition, this duality of time periods, the Fascist era in Italy and the 1960s in the United States is reiterated in another novel of the author, written, coincidentally, during the same historic time period: *Graffiti*.[8] In her essay, "Texts Within the Text: Hermeneutics of the 'Fluid' Novel *Benedetta in Guysterland* for the Jabberwocky Reader," Romana Capek-Habekovic, explains that there is a similarity between the two narratives. According to Capek-Habekovic, an understanding of *Graffiti* is necessary for the conception and under-

---

[8] Giose Rimanelli, *Graffiti*, edited by Titina Sardelli (Isernia: Editrice Marinelli, 1977).

standing of *Benedetta*. The former narrative laid the foundation for the structural and linguistic development of the novel's discourse in the latter.[9] Luigi Fontanella believes that the language experimentalism of the two novels deal with the linguistic word-play elements that the author reveals in these two texts and that he will further evolve in his forthcoming novel *Detroit Blues*.[10] Fontanella further elaborates on the linguistic elements by stating that Rimanlli's purpose is:

> Letteratura come Gioco e Gioco della Letteratura; giocare provocatoriamente con le parole e farsi gioco di esse, ma mettendosi, l'autore stesso, in gioco. (166)

These words, moreover, echo those of Piero Lapulce, protagonist of the novel *Graffiti*, who describes the metaphor as a game of words: "La metafora è un gioco di parole, ed è alla base della poesia. Se lo scopo dell'arte è quello di liberarci dalle repressioni, e se la civiltà è essenzialmente repressiva, allora l'arte è sovversione della civiltà" (40).

Detroit Blues,[11] as well as *Graffiti*, makes use of the interplay between these two separate universes, World War II and the 60s. However, in this novel, presented as a murder mystery, the author recounts the racial riots that took place in the city, in 1967, and lasted one week. It involves one Molisan family (Simone Donato and his relatives) and the two dissimilar generations (one, the immigrant from the Old World; and the other, the children of these refugees and, therefore, native born to the New World), within the

---

[9] Romana Capek-Habekovic, "Texts Within the Text: Hermeneutics of the "Fluid" Novel *Benedetta in Guysterland* for the Jabberwocky Reader" in *Rimanelliana*, edited by Sebastiano Martelli (Stony Brook: FILibrary, 2000) 204.

[10] Luigi Fontanella, "La narrativa in inglese di Giose Rimanelli," *Rivista di Studi Italiani* 19, (June 2001): 165.

[11] Giose Rimanelli, *Detroit Blues* (Welland, Ontario: Editions Soleil, 1997).

dynamic of this social group. The novel, ultimately, brings to light the devastation that divided a country politically and the cultural schism that existed between White and Black America.[12]

Rimanelli's novel *Graffiti*, written in Italian as is *Detroit Blues*, tells the story of Piero Lapulce, a young Molisan man falsely accused of the beating death of his landlady in Torino. During the police interrogation, the reader learns of his and his family's tragic personal history that initiates during World War II, before his birth, and continues into the present moment. As in this novel, *Benedetta in Guysterland*, there is a socio-political combination of the Italian Civil War and the civil unrest of the 1960s. Rimanelli, making use of his medieval literary tradition, interweaves classic Italian literary references within the text to create a fresh and biting satire of the sexual political dynamics of the period and the ever-changing role of women in the contemporary culture, as I have demonstrated elsewhere.[13] Capek-Habekovic points out that the graffiti proclamations that the protagonist utters as he, ultimately, is set free from prison, refers to and suggests other literary texts by other authors and in other mediums. "They are," according to Capek-Habekovic, "immersed in general literary discourse-ultimately in culture itself" (206).

Benedetta in Guysterland, like its Italian contemporary *Graffiti*, evokes other literary texts and it is within the specificity of the narrative that the reader perceives the intermingling of these outside elements. The author, in his *For-a-word*, informs the reader, from the start, that the novel is composed with intertextual components:

---

[12] See my "Road Signs Down a Path of Non Sequiturs in *Graffiti*," in *Crossing the Acheron: A Study of Nine Novels by Giose Rimanelli* (New York: Legas, 2000) 127-145.

[13] *Crossing the Acheron*, 147-167.

> This ballad *Benedetta* has been made up by the careful use of famous and infamous quotations, scraps of personal *co co rico co co rico* lyrics, confessions of country girls with kitsch and poetry pap, advertisements, newspaper and magazine lines, TV commercials, FBI or MGM releases, interviews, new books, old books read and digested, cartoon-blurbs ... (28)

The manipulation and incorporation of external sources is neither uncommon nor unique to the Rimanelli opus. All of his works, starting with *Tiro al piccione*, and continuing through the 1950s to today, incorporates the subtle use of the medieval classics and specifically the works of Dante, Petrarca and Boccaccio appear within the subtext of all his narratives.[14] If, as suggested, *Graffiti* has a parallel linguistic and structural development as *Benedetta*, then the appearance of the major Italian medievalists and philosophers in the earlier Italian novel would suggest that it would not be uncharacteristic for them to appear in this English novel of the author.

Rimanelli's novels of the 1950s, a decade that the author describes as "his time,"[15] deal with man's abuse of power and its ensuing consequences in a political, social, economic, and cultural post war-torn Italy. They serve as a foundation and an indication to the anecdotal process and evolution that expand, geometrically, within this truly experimental, first time English novel for this Italian born narrator. *Benedetta in Guysterland*, like its Italian literary precursors by this author, grapples with the exploitation of human supremacy over man's fear and loathing of a competing social group, however, now in a new era and in a new geographic location. The geopolitics of the era have transformed and taken on the battle cry of the war between the generations. In Rimanelli's tale the perversion is shown to exist, as in his earlier Italian narratives, within the political, com-

---

[14] I refer the reader once more to my *Crossing the Acheron*, 17-167.
[15] Conversations with the author, the most recent: 18 April 2006.

munal, fiscal and enlightening realms of the contemporary period, the 1960s, and it is manifested by the cultural-political conflict that takes place in the United States due to the American participation in the Vietnam War.

During the 1950s, Rimanelli wrote and published, within a period of less than ten years, five books: *Tiro al piccione*; *Peccato originale*; *Biglietto di terza*; *Una posizione sociale*; and *Il mestiere del furbo*.[16] Each of these tales, narrated in a traditional format, handle the socioeconomic and political oppression of the time that its characters endure while showing, simultaneously, their Orphic journey through the dark days of their existence in a universe that imparts very little hope of salvation. *Tiro al piccione,* Rimanelli's first book, offers the reader the story of a young boy who fights on the wrong side of the Italian Civil War and who witnesses man's maltreatment of his fellow man in a fratricidal ceremony that plays out *in illo tempore*; *Peccato originale* handles the poverty of a post civil war period in which the inhabitants of a small, southern community must emigrate to the New World because of their inability to progress, financially and socially, in a closed environment; *Biglietto di terza* depicts the arduous life of the immigrant, from his embarkation in the Old World, to his collective and financial establishment in the New World; *Una posizione sociale* portrays the social inequalities that exist in Italy during the prewar years by comparing it to the post civil war years in the United States; and *Il mestiere del furbo* tackles the ill-usage of authority within the confines of the literary and artistic world.

The vigilant reader of the novels of Rimanelli is acutely aware of

---

[16] *Tiro al piccione* (Milan: Mondadori, 1953; [Turin: Einaudi, 1991]); *Peccato originale* (Milan: Mondadori, 1954); *Biglietto di terza* (Milano: Mondadori Editore, 1958); *Una posizione sociale* (Florence: Vallechi Editore, 1959); and *Il mestiere del furbo* (Milan: Sugar, 1959).

the authenticity in each of these aforementioned narratives and perceives their presence, blended and integrated, punctuated within this new fable of *Benedetta in Guysterland*. The atrocities of the Italian Civil War that Marco Laudato suffers in *Tiro al piccione* are reverberated within this new text. Italian Fascism and its totalitarian form of government forces the Lavanda family (Joseph Adonis and his cousin, Santo, Zip the Thunder, Tristano) of Paliermu to forcibly leave Italy.

There is, moreover, a curious similarity in Benedetta's description of being locked in a room (searching for Joe), to Marco Laudato's being shut within his parents home, yet protected from the hostile German forces that are passing through his hometown:

> Dalla finestra osservavo tutto ciò che avveniva sulla strada....
> Col naso appiccicato ai vetri guardavo quel traffico. Mia madre ciabattava per la casa nella sua vestaglietta nera, ma infine, con la sua voce lontana, diceva:
> Levati una buona volta da quei vetri. Sei come una statua, non fai che guardare... (37)

Additionally, parallels can be made between *Benedetta in Guysterland* and Rimanelli's other narratives of the 1950s. The postwar period can be applicable to *Peccato originale*; the illegal entry of Zip the Thunder and Joseph Adonis indicates, like the book *Biglietto di terza* (although, in *Benedetta*, a varied means by which the immigrant made entry into America), a method of introduction into a new culture; unlawful activities in America, and the horrors of the prewar years in Italy, are the basis for the author's novel, *Una posizione sociale*; and the extreme negative behavior in the cultured world of literature, by the elder generation toward their new, younger contemporaries, who refuse to play the power games of previous years or be manipulated and controlled by others, is shown to be at the heart of *Mestiere del furbo*.

A divergent element, however, enters into *Benedetta* not witnessed in any of Rimanelli's other books. The protagonist is not from Molise, not Italian, nor a descendent of anyone from this small Appeninne region. Benedetta is from a small town called Appalachia. Yet, ironically, much like the other protagonists' home area in the author's previous books, Appalachia is located in the mountainous regions of mid-America, while Molise, coincidentally, is in the central part of the Italian peninsula in the Matese mountain range. There is a similarity of geographic characteristics within the framework of the author's previous compositions and the present narrative. Furthermore, the description of lifestyles in this small rural community of the United States is similar to the one that the author attributes to his home area in Italy. Appalachia, like Molise, is geographically separated, and distant, from all major cities thereby forming a world unto itself. Simultaneously, there is a similar sonorousness, musicality and vibrancy between the names of the two locations: Appalachia and Appenninno.

Traditionally, Molise has operated as the author's consecrated zone. According to Eliade, the sacred is tantamount to an unworldly power and to a divine reality.[17] In Rimanelli's novels of the 1950s, while the author's parents still resided in Italy, Molise operated as this consecrated area. However, once the writer's family immigrated to America, first to Canada and then to the United States, Detroit eventually became the new sacrosanct domain. In addition, within the sacred space of Molise or Detroit, Rimanelli's parents' home constituted that which Eliade further denominated as, the *axis*

---

[17] Mircea Eliade, *The Sacred and The Profane*, translated by Willard R. Trask (San Diego, New York, London: HBJ Book, 1959) 12.

"A Cracked Mirror, A Fragmented History"

mundi, the center of the universe.[18] Profane space would, therefore, institute anything that subsisted outside the chosen, consecrated area. In Rimanelli's novels, each time a character (Marco Laudato in *Tiro al piccione*; Nicola Vietri in *Peccato originale*; Massimo Niro in *Una posizione*) left the confines of the parents' home, the sacred space, the protagonist was confronted with the venomous and cruel realism of civil war, hatred, bigotry and violence.

For this young woman, Appalachia, like Molise in the other novels of the writer, operates as her sacred space. It is an area, according to Benedetta, primordial in behavior and in speech. Words are superfluous, as "useless as speaking to a tree" (86). It is described as a *locus amenus* of Mid America in which the people appear to be patterned after the nature that surrounds them. Within the boundaries of this consecrated area, her family house, functions as the *axis mundi* of her confined reality. In this center of her universe she learns about life from her father, a person to whom she attributes divine like properties.[19] Everything outside the realm of her esteemed Appalachia is profane space and it is in this desecrated area that the reality of the outside world, violence and war, makes its appearance, when she departs the area and goes to Anabais College.

The name of this institute of higher education, Anabais, reminds the reader of the classic work of Greek literature by Xenophon. Al-

---

[18] Mircea Eliade, *Images and Symbols: Studies in Religious Symbolism* (New York: Sheed and Ward, 1969) 39.

[19] "And it is in this relation that now I think of my father, a strong man under his quietness which would seem to the stranger a curtain of shyness. My father the Keeper, made of heavy tweed and the smell of pipe tobacco blending with the sweet perfume of a wood fire that burns in the fireplace in his study during the winter evenings. My father the big Man, although now only his hands and feet show his size as his body is beginning to shrink in the eternal cold. My father with the long ears of an Easter Island Aku-Aku statue, in his domain, a room filled with books, papers, the smell of a wood fire and tobacco smoke. My father and his feet..." (87-88).

though the tale narrates the story of a large Greek army of 10,000 mercenaries hired by Cyrus the Younger to seize, from his brother Artaxerex II, the throne of Persia, the term itself has come to refer to a long journey. Benedetta, speaking of the College, states:

> The college prepares anyone for the world and its oddities. It is a shocking place for the freshmen who come starry-eyed and eager to learn about life and how to be wicked. (135)

Anabais College, like its namesake, will offer the young Benedetta a voyage, not only away from the safety of her parents' house and the sanctity of New Wye, but will take her down a path to a new and more profound understanding of life and the realities of the time. It will open her eyes to the brutality and cruelty of humanity that exists outside the realm of her enclosed provenance and show her the violence that is occurring in the world at large.

In *Benedetta in Guysterland*, a pseudo *axis mundi*, a type of sanctuary, develops for this young woman within the profane space she encounters once she departs her home town of New Wye. This new area is the small room above the nightclub in which Zip the Thunder is holding her captive in New Jersey. It is from this room that all information regarding the lives of the two opposing families, and her, is disseminated. It is, also, from here that time mutates and realities of the present amalgamate with the actualities of the past. Old and new ways of life share the confines of this small abode. At the same time, the story of the *Ballad Benedetta* is reminiscent of King Solomon's *Song of Songs*. In Solomon's tale, as in the case of Benedetta, the king (Zip the Thunder) is the rival of affection for the young maiden (Benedetta) of a shepherd. Solomon carries off the beautiful young girl and brings her to Jerusalem where he endeavors to win her affection. She resists and remains faithful to her country lover (Joe Adonis). Ultimately, she is reunited with him.

"A Cracked Mirror, A Fragmented History"

The reader is prompted, by the enclosed room in which Benedetta is imprisoned, of a poem that this author writes, more than 15 years after *Benedetta in Guysterland*, which resonates and forms a type of undercurrent, a hymn, within the text:

> Sono chiuso in una stanza
> piccolino come il mondo.
> Rido e danzo, a volte piango,
> sono intenso come il mondo.
> Alla fine, rassegnato
> ho sposato l'emozione.[20]

At the close of his *For-a-word*, the author presents us his "Ballad Benedetta". The musical composition is suggested from the narrative's inception. The relationship between his *Ballad Benedetta* and the *Ballad of Joe Selimo* (from which the above stanza appears) is the musicalness and construction of the words in each of the texts; its fundamental morphologic components. In the introduction to his translation of Rimanelli's *Moliseide*, Luigi Bonaffini explains that *Moliseide* is a collection of ballads and songs. An overriding element, according to Bonaffini, in Rimanelli's ballads is repetition, from the phonetic to the structural. He adds:

> Yet the importance of the refrain in *Moliseide* is also grounded on another fundamental, but less distant, derivation: the refrain is the basic structural element of another mode of accentual oral poetry and song called "The Blues", in which repetition does not play a merely decorative or expressive role, and it too is a return to origins, and one of the most influential musical genre of the century. A genre with which Rimanelli is well acquainted, having himself written in the past several blues and jazz pieces, whose lifeblood now courses through

---

[20] Giose Rimanelli, "Ballata di Joe Selimo" in *Moliseide: Songs and Ballads in the Molisan Dialect*, translated by Luigi Bonaffini (New York: Peter Lang, 1992) 48.

and nourishes many of these dialect compositions, some of which bear titles that are as revealing as they are technically appropriate. (xxxi-xxxii)

Music has, in the works of Rimanelli, played an underlying and groundbreaking function. *Una posizione sociale,* which tells the story of the 1891 lynching of Italians in New Orleans, incorporates the American genre of jazz both within the text, as a premise for the grandfather's odd nocturnal behavior, and in the physical appearance of a 45 disc. The music serves as more than a backdrop for the story. It becomes an integral part of the narrative. Years later, the author's book, *Familia,*[21] also makes use of this unique American art form, jazz. In the text, Rimanelli points out the dichotomous nature of this artistic creation by showing that the birth of jazz, although traced to a traditional African American phenomenon, became popularized by a Caucasian band known as the *Original Dixieland Jazz Band.*[22]

Now, in *Benedetta in Guysterland,* jazz no longer plays the dominant character that it has in the other novels of the author, but the lyrics of many contemporary rock songs, placed strategically within the text, have an overpowering role. The melodies serve as a segue between the various temporal moments of the narrative and to show the futility of war:

"I've never listened to music like this before ... I'm hearing so much more intensely with my outer ear ... and yet ... at the same time I'm lis-

---

[21] Giose Rimanelli, *Familia* (Isernia: Iannone, 2000).
[22] In January 2001, the *PBS* network presented a documentary, *Jazz,* on the history of this purely American music phenomenon, produced by Ken Burns. According to the program, although jazz music was a creation of the African American community that had its origins, in some form or another, during the Antebellum days, the La Rocca band was, actually, the first to produce, in 1917, a recorded disc for sale on the market.

tening with my inner ear ... I hear melodies ... and melodies in the melodies. I hear Tchaikovsky himself! And I can see it all too! The melody passes before my eyes ... I see ... I see centuries and all of the glory and the tragedy of guys ... Everything is in this music! ... But especially the tragedy of guys. (106)

Capek-Habekovic states that the implanting of literary and non-literary matter, as well as from other media sources, contributes to the chronological and spatial frame the narrative needs to be understood (210). Music becomes, therefore, the metaphor for the difference between the warring families in this saga and it extends to the nation as a whole. However, it is the lyrics, the words of these tunes, which becomes the allegory of the narration.

The songs interlaced within this narrative frame of the text are indicative of a negative socio-political-cultural progression taking place in the nation, that is tearing it apart, and, that the young Joe Adonis is trying to amend: a dishonorable and pointless war in Vietnam. The author plays with the lyrics of contemporary songs such as the anti-war protest melody, *War* (Edwin Starr), *Evil Ways* (Santana), *Fire and Rain* (James Taylor) and concludes with John Lennon's bittersweet anthem for a better world, *Imagine*. The lyrics of these songs define a generation. Unlike their parents who fought in a war because they were physically attacked due to their political principles (nationality, religion, culture), this younger community perceives that war in Southeast Asia is unjust and unethical. They believe that the government, the older generation, is attempting to impose their culture, as the aggressors did in World War II, on another society. The young attack this aggressive philosophy, not physically or brutally, but with the use of language, a much more subtle and effective tool.

From the novel's introduction, through the entire text, and eventually, to the *Post-Word*, the role that language plays within the con-

"A Cracked Mirror, A Fragmented History"

fines of this novel is paramount. The lyrics of the tunes are the external stimuli that bring the reader back to the beginning of the narrative and remind the reader of the grandness and power of the word. From its inception, Rimanelli uses musical terminology to explain the function of language:

> As dada rock gets worse, outdoor micro-boppers get better. (27)

and, although the author states that he doesn't understand, there are two opposing musical genres within the statement: rock, the music of the contemporary period; and boppers, the music of the World War II era, each separate and different from the other; each involved in a political conflict of opposing realities. Moreover, the music of the 1960s served as a type of national hymn for the antiwar movement, whereas the music of the World War II era functioned to remind the soldiers of home and hearth and the reason for which they are fighting a war: freedom of political doctrines and personal and cultural ideas.

Classic literature has, according to Rimanelli, been a source for his literary experience. In the preface to his book *Moliseide*, a collection of 100 poems written in his native Molisan dialect and in Italian, the author states, regarding this collection of poetry, that:

> If the *Aeneid* sings the glory, we sing our everyday passions: love, pain, anger, the quarrel, the reconciliation, the dirty trick, the distant land, dreams, desires, ghost - and not to make immortal art as Virgil did (almost impossible nowadays, times being what they are, and ironically given the label of *post-modernism*) but pop-pap. Even with this the memory of your roots can be saved. (xix)

Bonaffini further elucidates that in *Moliseide*, a book that the author defines as an epic journey, Rimanelli has the compulsion to return to literary sources that are bound up with his cultural background (xxvii).

However, here in *Benedetta in Guysterland,* the author takes the classic European literature and interweaves it with the popular culture of the day, specifically the music and lyrics of a generation, and creates a post-modern labyrinthine reality in which the words of the songs take the listener on a journey through the horrors and the futility of a new political conflict: the war in Vietnam.

To bring out the absurdity of war the author creates within this narrative a situation that parallels the story of Cain and Abel and, at the same time, creates a parody of huge proportions with the idea of a mafia-like, family organization in which fratricide, or any homicide, is not uncommon and looked upon as a badge of honor. In his preface to the novel, Fred Gardaphé states that *Benedetta in Guysterland* has a critical place in the history of Italian American literature. He explains that this text functions as the bridge between modernism and postmodernism of the Italian American narrative. Moreover, Gardaphé additionally, points out that this is the first Italian American novel to parody accepted Italian American culture (14-15). Brunella Bigi, in her essay "Ethnicity and its Discontent: Reading Italians in Multicultural Societies", reverberates Gardaphé's thesis that *Benedetta in Guysterland* is a parody. She adds, however, that the spoof is the sentimental relationship that exists between Italy and America and that it is achieved through the demythologization of stereotypes that unite the two countries.[23] In his most recent study on *Benedetta,* written more than ten years after the original introduction to the book, Gardaphé exams Rimanelli's use of male sexuality to undermine the power of the traditional gangster by turning

---

[23] Brunella Bigi, "Ethnicity and Its Discontent: Reading Italians in Multicultural Societies," in *Voices in Italian Americana* 10.1 (1999): 18-19.

his potency into impotence.[24]

The story of the Gelatari war, between two Sicilian families in New York, is told to us, as summarized from a book, by Benedetta. Each of these families came from the same small town in Italy and each was attempting to be more powerful than the other. The internal hostilities that initiated in New York spread throughout the country. Families in other locales were taking sides on the results of this gangland terror. Simultaneously, each of these groups was a victim of the tyrannical and oppressive politics in Italy, headed by the notorious Muscolini, who refused to be part of any of the bands that, ultimately, brought the now, present day leaders of the *banda* to the United States. More important, according to this history, Zip the Thunder and Joseph Adonis, the father of Joe, are cousins, thereby creating a blood relationship between Joe and Zip.

This saga, told while Benedetta is held captive in a room above a night club called *La Gaia Scienza*, reminds the reader, as Anthony Julian Tamburri submits, of Friedrich Nietzsche's *Die Fröhliche Wissenschaft, The Gay Science*, or Giambattista Vico's opus entitled *La Nuova Scienza*.[25] Vico's theory is, basically, that history is repetitive and that human culture is divided into three cycles: divine, heroic, and human. If, as Tamburri alludes, although never elucidates, there is a possible influence of the philosophy of Vico and the cyclical nature of the past, then the unfortunate and devastating cosmos of war and its constant repetition, *illo tempore*, is the component that abounds in this novel. At the same time, this possible allusion to Vico's work reinstates Rimanelli's passion for the classic

---

[24] Fred L. Gardaphé, *From Wiseguys to Wise Men: The Gangster and Italian American Masculinities* (New York and London: Routledge, 2006) 89.

[25] Anthony Julian Tamburri, "*Benedetta in Guysterland*: Postmodernism [Pre-]Visited," in *Rimanelliana*, edited by Sebastiano Martelli (Stony Brook: FILibrary, 2000) 238.

fonts within his work.

The personal story of the author's participation in Italy's Civil War is not limited to his first book, *Tiro al piccione*. It is a tragic saga that goes beyond this original tale and is echoed in many of the Rimanelli's narratives including *Graffiti*, *Il tempo nascosto tra le righe*,[26] in which Marco Laudato, the protagonist of *Tiro al piccione*, re-appears in the contemporary period, some 30 years after the war, *Familia*, and his most recent narrative, *Il viaggio*.[27] Each of these novels transports the reader back and forth between two very distinct eras: the contemporary period in America and the war years in Europe. All of these texts bring to light the social and political unrest of a nation and, *Il viaggio*, the most recent of the author's books, points an accusatory finger, specifically, at President Bush's erroneous foreign policy and the unethical reasons for which the country is at war in Iraq.

René Girard explains that physical ferocity can be a hallowed act. He states; "violence is the heart and soul of the sacred."[28] According to Girard, murder without forfeiture is the ultimate sacrosanct act because it is the reincarnation of the Cain and Abel's story. The sanctity lies in that the sacrificial victim is forgotten and replaced by a surrogate victim (5). Abel, the shepherd, had an offering to give to G-d; Cain, the farmer, did not. Cain gave up his brother in anger.[29] Therefore if, as Girard points out, brutality were a hallowed act, then war, civil war, would be an action that transports man back *in illo tempore*.

Mircea Eliade explains that a myth relates a sacred history, a

---

[26] Giose Rimanelli, *Il tempo nascosto tra le righe* (Isernia: Marinelli Editore, 1986).
[27] Giose Rimanelli, *Il viaggio* (Isernia: Iannone, 2003).
[28] René Girard, *Violence and the Sacred*, translated by Patrick Gregory (Baltimore and London: The John Hopkins University Press, 1989) 31.
[29] *Genesis* 4:1-9.

primal occurrence that took place *ab initio*. The parable is history that took place, *in illo tempore*. Once told, the mystery becomes an unconditional legitimate action; it constitutes a validity that is unequivocal.[30] If, however, as Eliade states, myth is always the recital of a creation and it speaks only of realities, then the myth that Rimanelli is trying to uncover is the brutality and foolishness of war.

Temporal repositioning occurs, one evening, in which Zip the Thunder, talks about an episode of the television series *Gunsmoke*. Zip describes an installment of the series in which the hero, Matt Dillon, saves the saloon-keeper, Miss Kitty, from being attacked and raped by another man. The images and dialogue of the episode create a frame-like narrative structure to the reality that blends when Zip, discussing the manner by which he became associated with the family, also describes his first encounter with the woman who would become the mother of his nemesis, Joe Adonis.

Television, however, takes on the metaphorical aspect of the realism in the outside world and, simultaneously, the exterior reality takes on the realness of television, verifying the statement of Fish, one of Zip's crew, who states, "TV is a great mass-media university." (p. 56) Truth and fiction have crisscrossed and combined into one for Zip: watching the television show in which the sheriff is able to save the day, kill the bad guy and still go home with the pretty girl illustrates the dual nature of man and his generation: "life is divided into two parts, business and pleasure, war and peace." (p. 58) This brutal episode on television contrasts vividly with the reality that is happening outside his domicile in which the young are protesting the violence abroad:

> The optimist asserts it as a possibility of achievement of Word Peace because all guys are brothers. The pessimist cites sibling rivalry. The

---

[30] *The Sacred and The Profane*, 95.

idealist declares guy's basic religious bonds will draw him into one peaceful community. The realist cites United Arab Republic's Allah and Israel's G-d. The alarmist pleads nuclear bombs must make war unthinkable. The Stoic says, "What guy can imagine, guy can do." Meanwhile, the neighborhood kids are throwing rocks at each other like little devils; the students are storming the administration building at college; and two countries such as New Jersey an the Bronx are massing their instrumental armies at the border ..." (58-59)

The binary pathway created between television and the war in Vietnam has intermingled and blended into one absolute truth for Zip. The war is justifiable and it is acceptable because it corrects, as Zip perceives, an unexplainable evil, as told to him via television images. Zip does not question the authority of these visualizations. They have become truth by their mere presence on the television screen. Joe, on the other hand, considers the Vietnam War an immoral undertaking. He believes that it is better not to fight than to commit an unlawful activity. Above all, Joe is capable of separating these two diverse elements: reality and fiction. He understands that they do not necessarily form one large picture, but rather two distinct visions, each distinguished from one another.

Benedetta's transcendental journey in time commences the first night she is held captive by Zip in the room above the nightclub. She does not understand the reason for which her great love, Joe Adonis, has been exiled. She describes her experience as a dream like state when she says "My sleep deceives me." (71) The journey that the protagonist makes, in her hypnogogic state, is one that agrees with Eliade's concept of *dream time*: a return to the start, *ab initio*, of creation; man must re-create the myth, *in illo tempore*, of his own beginnings (*imago mundi*). *Dream time* empowers man to reincorporate the sacred time of the commencement of things, and, therefore, to renew the world.[31] The illusion will permit Benedetta to distinguish the rudiments that form the conflict between Zip and Joe. At the same time, it will allow her to realize, as Joe did in an earlier time, that there is a huge schism between verity and prevarication and that it is language, its proper use that makes it possible to maneuver this gulf.

In archaic societies, according to Eliade, young men must pass a rite of initiation in which the first stage of this procedure is the detachment of the neophyte from his mother. This severance, sometimes violent, is a split with the world of childhood; the apprentice essentially embarks upon the sacred universe of adulthood. The disclosure of the sacred means that the young man, in a short amount of time, interprets the whole body of his cultures' mythological and humanizing customs. Furthermore, the transition from the profane world to the sacred suggests an experience of death: the destruction of one life for another. If, as Eliade states, the maternal universe is the profane world, then breaking away from it, even demolishing it, would be a sacred act (3-9).

The initiation rite would have to bring the novice into the sacred world of human sacrifice, the act that transports him back *ab initio* and, eventually, to the re-enactment of the myth of Cain and Abel, epitomized, in contemporary society, by civil war. Joe refuses to participate in any physical hostility, even though his mother, from whom he must separate, according to the theories of Eliade, believes that; "chi nasce tondo non muore quadro," (58) suggesting that ferocity is a primordial endeavor that conveys the individual back to its origin, *imago mundi*. She anticipates Joe will, like everyone else, ultimately, accept the reality of the existent world with its tangible

---

[31] Mircea Eliade, *Rites and Symbols of Initiation*, Translated from the French by Willard R. Trask (New York, Hagerstown, San Francisco, London: Harper Torchbooks, 1958) 6.

universe as shown on television. He, therefore, according to his mother, will do the militant and unavoidable act: take part in a war for which he does not accept the political foundation, because the visualization that he witnesses will pass through and enter into the actual world. By rejecting, however, his mother's view of the world, Joe has broken from the profane cosmos and this rupture suggests that he has, therefore, performed a revered feat. At the same time, Benedetta will learn to distinguish fact from fiction. This enterprise will be accomplished with her metaphysical trek that progresses through the ages.

The journey through these two disparate universes is one that transports the reader back in time to witness the immorality of man through the ages. Benedetta, additionally, informs the reader, just before entering into her dream state, that "A grotesquerie of chaotic nightwails. Border guards at the hell's gate." (51) This indication allows the reader to clearly perceive the infernal trek that is about to commence. It is an Orphic voyage on which Benedetta embarks when she is held captive and Zip remands her to a room above the nightclub:

> And he said to me: 'Some stones are still warm. A ghost can whistle. But nowhere is out. I saw the cold.'
> And sent me upstairs, in the past. Just a narrow room with naked neon blasts. A dream at the moment of begetting. (41)

This passage prompts the reader to remember Dante's entrance into *Inferno* when the poet, awakening from his sleep, finds himself looking upward to the light and the path that would, eventually, taken him out of the ravine of hell and lead him to the elevation of paradise.[32]

---

[32] *Inferno* I: 1-18.

The presence of Dante and his journey in the works of Rimanelli is not without precedence, as I have demonstrated elsewhere,[33] and here in *Benedetta in Guysterland*, it is exceptionally clear within the specificity of the text. The precise reference to Dante appears, midway through the narrative when Zip the Thunder is telling Benedetta the manner in which Joe first came to be famous. According to Zip, Joe would leave the city, visit friends afar, and "would read Dante to the lepers." (p. 94). The reference to Dante permits a direct correlation to the author's statement in the prologue in which he states that his story is "A mad journey far from himself." (29)

According to Dante and the medieval tradition, the number three is of great importance and consequence. Christopher Ryan, in his essay *The Theology of Dante*, explains the solemnity of the number:

> For Dante, the striving of the human being both to come to individual perfection in knowledge and love, and to reach the perfection in and through a community, *has* its source in the already perfect life of the Trinity.[34]

Structurally, there are three parts to this novel *Benedetta in Guysterland* that jump between three distinct time frames: the modern day era; the World War II period; and, in the final analysis, the return to *ab initio* as a primary source of the bad animus between Joe Adonis and Zip the Thunder. Benedetta discusses three of the major lovers in her life: Joe, the most recent; Willie "Holiday Inn" Sinclair who was her first link to the Lavanda family and who was, ulti-

---

[33] I refer the reader yet again to my *Crossing the Acheron,* passim.
[34] Christopher Ryan, "The Theology of Dante," in *The Cambridge Companion to Dante,* edited by Rachel Jacoff (Cambridge: Cambridge University Press, 1993) 151.

mately, "kissed" by Zip; and Jargon, who she called Sandboy, her first childhood boyfriend of any importance. There are three young women who have been students at Anabais College: Benedetta; Crystal Baby and Carolyn, both of whom left the institute shortly before Benedetta's arrival. At the same time, the life of Benedetta is divided into three major segments: her childhood in New Wye, Nabokov County, Appalachia (three geographic terms for her, one, home area); her life at Anabais College and her encounter with Joe Adonis and the *banda*; and the time after Joe's death, once set free by Zip the Thunder, and her acquaintanceship with the author. There are, moreover, references made to three distinct historical literary time epochs: the classic period of the Greeks; the Italian Renaissance; and the modern traditional narrative period, popularized by the nineteenth-century French novelist Flaubert, three distinct eras with three different and unique cultures. Coincidentally, Benedetta's transcendental journey into the various time periods originates in Chapter III. Equally important is that the title of the narrative is, simultaneously, comprised of three words.

The temporal journey of Benedetta is one that takes the reader through time and creates parallels with the present day reality of the war in Vietnam with, specifically, the Fascist era that brought the Italian peninsula into a Civil War. Rimanelli's *capolavoro*, of this gruesome period, is the story of Marco Laudato and his horrific war time experiences as portrayed in *Tiro al piccione*. Marco, at the start of the novel, is a 17 year old boy caught up in the fratricidal war of the country, fighting on the wrong side. However, by the time he returns home to Casacalenda, he is an 18 year old man.

The novel *Benedetta in Guysterland* was initiated 18 years after Marco fought in the Civil War (1943-1961). Benedetta, whose age is never fixed but easily calculated, is the same age as Marco when he started his voyage of awareness. Mathematically, Marco, the alter ego of the author, in 1961, is 35 years old and has reached the "mezzo del cammin di nostra vita," of Dante. Additionally, there are 18 years between the publication of Rimanelli's *Tiro al piccione* (1953) and the 1971 date of the ten-year period it took to create *Benedetta in Guysterland*.

There is in *Benedetta in Guysterland*, as there is in *Graffiti*, the novel that Rimanelli wrote during this same period with a similar linguistic game plan strategy, an arithmetic precision reminiscent of the Middle Ages.[35] There are 18 years between this novel and the author's first, *Tiro al piccione*. Divide the 18 years by the binary path established within the framework of this narrative and the number nine is the resultant; the identification number of circles in Dante's *Inferno*. Additionally, the square root of nine is three; the total number of parts in the Florentine's *Divina commedia* and, at the same time, the total quantity of structural elements that comprise this present day novel by Rimanelli.

Moreover, an historic literary relationship between *Tiro al piccione* and *Benedetta in Guysterland* may be established when Benedetta brings to light the history of the Lavanda family and the impossible coexistence between the family and the tyrannical leader Muscolini that forced their exile to the United States. Through the use of parody, Rimanelli, playing with the name of the Fascist dictator, Mussolini, reminds the reader of the horrors that his prototype hero endures. Equally important is that *Tiro al piccione* is the first Italian novel of the author and *Benedetta in Guysterland* is his first in English. As *Tiro al piccione* describes the horrors of the Italian Civil War, *Benedetta in Guysterland* relates a parallel story, the Gelatari War, by describing yet another Italian civil war: the infamous history of the Castellemmarese War (1928-1931) that takes place

---

[35] See my *Crossing the Acheron*, 149-150.

within the United States. Rimanelli's new novel paints a portrait of brutality and animosity within America that corresponds to the Black Shirt terrorism tactics of Mussolini a few years earlier.

At the same time, the novel progresses into the latter half of the twentieth century and the author brings to light, within the boundaries of the United States, the civil war atmosphere, in the contemporary period, to a new political reality: the War in Vietnam. In a conversation with Benedetta during a dream sequence, Joe suggests that he is "semantic" and that "geniality is deconstruction."

> But, what is geniality, Benedetta? And if geniality does not exist, then, what is roadside?
> I do not know, Joe!
> I love you. I shall always love you with as much tenderness and as strongly as I once loved those weird objects that my intolerance found pleasure in creating, those dreams of which a part of your geniality is made. In fact, it is solely his imagination that can provide guy with the only kind of positive geniality that he is capable of obtaining. It is true wisdom to seek this geniality in deconstruction, I think.
> Yes, Joe! (78)

If deconstruction is the basis of Joe's discourse, then the reconstruction of the combined elements within the novel suggest a new and varied manner in which to exhibit the present day reality.

Zip, according to Benedetta, is in charge of the family. He is the "Boss of all Bosses" (102) of the unified Commission. As television takes on the analogical panorama of the real world for Zip and his associates, the family, the *banda*, becomes the metaphor of the Legislature Branch of the United States Government to Joe and his colleagues. The head of this family, therefore, is the Executive Office of the President, with all his absolute powers that can either take a nation into a disastrous war or into a period of blessed peace.

Dante's voyage across the Acheron, the first major step in his

"A Cracked Mirror, A Fragmented History"

journey out of *Inferno,* was in a small boat. During this passage, however, he is accompanied by his guide, Virgil, the poet that "Nacqui sub Iulio" (*Inferno* I: 70) and who is known, as the Florentine points out, for "quella fonte che spandi di parlar sì largo fiume?" (*Inferno* I: 79-80). Although the reader finds out that Zip and his crew have "kissed" the "Little Virgilian," Virgil, the great Latin poet and guide to Dante on his voyage through *Inferno* plays a substantial persona in this narrative and it is perceived within the subtext.

In a variation of the dantean concept, Rimanelli presents a guide through the contemporary socio political period whose family history spans the two geopolitical time frames of the modern era, the territorial power struggle in Europe and the one in America: Joe Adonis. This name suggests, moreover, the dichotomy of the text. Joe, the typical American name attributed to the World War II soldier who fought in Europe for social and political freedom, and Adonis, the Greek hero of classic mythology who spends his eternity in the dark underworld after being gored by a boar, loved by two women: Aphrodite and Persephone.

Virgil's last work, the *Aeneid*, serves as a literary source for Rimanelli's tale of *Benedetta in Guysterland,* as he stated in his previsouly cited preface to *Moliseide*. Rimanelli's story of Joe and his conflict with the Lavanda family is a variation on Virgil's story of the epic hero, Aeneas. In the classic tale, after escaping the sacking of Troy, Aeneas heads towards Italy. On his voyage to the peninsula, a storm brings him to the coast of Carthage, where he meets and falls in love, magically, with Dido. Jupiter, however, recalls Aeneas to military duty forcing him to abandon Dido, who curses him for discarding her. On arriving in Italy, the Cumaean Sibyl conducts him through the Underworld and reveals his destiny to him. He is, in the end, reborn the creator of Imperial Rome. Virgil's story of Aeneas has him struggling between doing what he wants to do as a man, and doing what he must as a virtuous hero.

In this contemporary version of the saga, the fable is reversed. Joe, according to *guy tradition*, is supposed to fight in the war.[36] He is to be a member of the "cosmopolitan underworld", headed by Zip the Thunder. Zip, like Jupiter (Zeus) with his thunderbolts and overwhelming power in the *banda*, recalls Joe to do battle. Zip, according to Benedetta, is running the show; he is in power. However, this hero refuses to take up arms; he declines to fight, and because of this, becomes the enemy of Zip and his Commission. Joe, contrary to Aeneas, believes it is more important to be morally justified in life as a man and, and not as a combatant. At the same time, war in both these fables, is the basis for the epic journey. Aeneas fights in his classic battle as Jupiter mandates; Joe, who is philosophically against the war in which Zip wants him to participate, fights a different battle, without ever shooting a gun: a war of words.

The passage across the Acheron allows Dante to bear witness to the various levels and degrees of those condemned to *Inferno*. It carries him, ultimately, to the ninth circle of Hell to encounter those damned to eternal darkness for their betrayal of mankind. The betrayers, according to Dante, are Judas, Brutes and Cassias, each of whom deceived their faith, their family, and their nation.

In a structural congruency of this novel with the work of the Florentine, Rimanelli's variation on the Orphic journey of his protagonist appears in a dream sequence that takes place in chapter IX.

---

[36] "Playing with a guy was something I *had* to do. I didn't have much choice in the matter. I didn't think about the whole thing and come to a decision. I was driven by needs which I didn't, and to a large extent still don't, understand. All I was aware of was that my needs for physical combat with a guy were both absolutely necessary to my life and contrary to *everything* I had ever been taught. And that's just my experience."

'You talk too much about yourself,' Zip said. 'To be a bandsman means to be committed, not to complain. Commitment is an act, not a word." (64)

"A Cracked Mirror, A Fragmented History"

Benedetta, after having escaped a sea monster who swallowed her up, is transported, like Dante across the Acheron, to the opposite side of a stream by a young fisherman.[37] Additionally, to further describe the underworld into which Benedetta has now entered in her dream like state, the author paints a portrait of her attempt to escape by comparing it to the English epic saga, *Beowulf,* and the story of the Dane and Grendel, the horrible demon who lives in the swampland of Hrothgar's kingdom. The guide for Benedetta on her journey out of the abyss is Joe, who like a Dante, has been exiled from his native country and informs the lost pilgrim:

> I'm crawling up a perpendicular concrete wall. When I look downwards I can see no bottom. Upwards there is no finish. The sides stretch out into infinity. There are no handholds but I am tired, and if I stop I will fall. I must keep climbing upwards then, like a fly on a wall. (79-80)

The fate of the voyagers, all travelers, is determined in the crossing of the Acheron. A person either descends further into the dark abyss or climbs up to the next level. Joe's description, more importantly, echoes Dante's of the autumnal season in which the trees along the Acheron lose their leaves and stand bare without anything for a person to grasp.[38] At the same time, Benedetta informs the

---

[37] "..A young fisherman has caught me in his net.... The serpent rises out of the water ... grown into a huge sea monster ... opens its jaws and snaps them shut on half of the fisherman's boat. With the next bit it will swallow both of us. A thunderbolt comes out of the sky and smashes the boat in two, leaving half of it stuck in the monster's gullet.
The fisherman takes me in his arms and swims with me towards shore.... The sea monster pursues us...." (75-77)

[38] "Come d'autunno si levan le foglie / l'una appresso de l'altra, fin che 'l ramo / vede a la terra tutte le sue spoglie, // similmente il mal seme d'Adamo / gittansi di quel lito ad una ad una, / per cenni come augel per suo richiamo." (*Inferno* III: 112-17)

reader that the immediate action of this internal war is taking place during the Halloween season, the middle of autumn, the period in which all trees are beginning to lose their foliage and enter into their dormant state.[39] Dante illustrates that the people who reside in *Inferno*, those who attempt to traverse this first river in Hell, are the "il mal seme d'Adamo." If, as Dante's states, those travelers are the "evil seed of Adam," then they would all have to be the descendants of Cain who, because of jealousy, killed his brother Abel, and, therefore, serves as the implicit comparison to civil war.

Moreover, the story of the relationship between Willie "Holiday Inn" Sinclair and Benedetta is strongly evocative of Dante's tale of Francesca and Paolo,[40] the two silent lovers who are killed by the husband of Francesca, Gianciotto, and once in hell where all adulterous people go, they are never separated. Rimanelli presents variations on the story by reversing the categorizations of several of the characters. As in the case of Francesca and Paolo who do not speak to each other and yet fall into passionate love, a similar scenario takes place between Benedetta and Willie. When the two first meet, they didn't communicate at all with each other,[41] but as time passed, they were inseparable and spend evenings together, unlike Francesca and Paolo, in long, constant conversations. However, in Ri-

---

[39] "Now, now. What to make of this Halloween goblin? This gilt-edged invitation to decadence, this life lived with constantly recurring visions of love, jail and sickness, laced with the beckoning insinuation of champagne and flaming foods, or Oriental rugs and dimly lit *bordelli*, surrounded by punkies and exotic friends like Anthony "little Pussy" Mosca, boss in Eaton, Pennsylvania and Larry Dogson, Lavanda chieftain, now in semi-retirement in Waterbury, Conn.?" (63)

[40] "Quando leggemmo il disïato riso / esser basciato da cotanto amante, / questi, che mai da me non fia diviso, // la bocca mi basciò tutto tremante. / Galeotto fu 'l libro e chi lo scrisse: / quel giorn più non vi leggemmo avante (*Inferno* V: 133-138).

[41] "The first time Willie and I were together alone, we didn't speak a word to each other. We sat and stared out at the water of the lake which glimmered in the later afternoon sun" (115).

manelli's tale, it is Willie who is married and not Benedetta.

Francesca and Paolo initiated their illicit affair while reading the *Galeotto*. In the original tale, Lancelot develops a warm friendship with Galeotto, who, upon finding out that Lancelot had feelings for Guinevere, arranged for a meeting between the two. Galeotto urged the Queen to kiss Lancelot and so began their affair. The variance in the relationship between Benedetta and Willie is that there was no go-between that united them in passion. Benedetta, however, was aware of her betrayal. Additionally, Willie's wife, Hester Prynne, had an affair prior to the relationship that develops between Benedetta and Willie. The name Hester Prynne reminds the reader of Nathaniel Hawthorne's novel *The Scarlet Letter*. In that book, Hester is mandated to wear the letter A, for adulteress, punishment for the crime of her unfaithfulness.

More crucial to the present day narrative is that Francesca tells Dante that her husband, Gianciotto, is destined to live, once dead, in Caina, for having killed her and his brother Paolo: "Caina, attende chi a vita ci spense" (*Inferno* V: 107). The underworld realm of Caina, according to Dante, is the first ring of the ninth circle of *Inferno* where, according to tradition, traitors of their consanguineous relatives are immersed in ice. Dante tells the story of Caina, so named for Cain, the biblical brother who killed his sibling, in Canto XXXII.

The story of Francesca and Paolo is, according to Teolinda Barolini, more than a story of lust. It deals, at the same time, with the political corruption of Florence.[42] Boccaccio explains, in his *Comento*, that the marriage between Francesa and Gianciotto was the groundwork to put an end to a long, harsh civil war, and to cement a bond between the two rival families: Francesca, the daughter of Guido Da

---

[42] Teolinda Barolini, "Dante and the Lyric Past," in *The Cambridge Companion to Dante*, 31.

Polenta the elder, lord of Ravenna and Cervia; and the Malatesta family, lords of Rimini.[43]

In Rimanelli's saga, the author plays with the same basic storyline when he has Zip the Thunder, kill Willie,[44] a family member, and therefore, as preordained by Dante's narrative, which is interwoven within this saga, destined to reside in the Ninth Circle of Hell. However, the author's story of *Benedetta in Guysterland* has the identical foundation for his narrative as the Florentine's: the political corruption of the period, the 1960s, that is forcing a country, the United States, to participate in an unjust war. Rimanelli, moreover, is pointing an accusatory finger at the Executive and Legislative Branches of the American government. He points out that they have betrayed their country by getting the nation involved in an unpardonable war.

The lines between the factions are easily discernable: those who believe that the government's justification for a military involvement in Vietnam is virtuous and those who believe that the war is just an unnecessary evil. Words, therefore, form the cornerstone for the war of governmental policy being played out in the country, in a non-ending battle between young and old. In an ironic understatement, moreover, the author illuminates that neither generation, the younger nor older, is communicating with the other and, therefore, as Francesca and Paolo are condemned to hell in an unspoken union, the American public is living in an infernal reality due to their

---

[43] As cited in, Dante Alighieri, *The Divine Comedy*, translated, with a Commentary by Charles S. Singleton, *Inferno, 2. Commentary* (Princeton: Princeton University Press, 1970) 97.

[44] "And Willie is dead now, because the chain he was in is the chain I am now in; and he is dead because the guys didn't like the way he used to talk. He was kissed down in a New Jersey restaurant because the Boss of all Bosses, Zip the Thunder, feared he would talk too much; and because he feared that Willie could not overcome his marriage problems; and because he failed to understand why Willie was attracted to young nymphets; and most of all feared that he would one day kiss him down in a street" (72).

generational silence.

The political hostilities that unfolds in the United States, due to this war, serves as the foundation for the linguistic word game pattern that the author presents in this novel. It extends far beyond the simple playing with the words and their intentions. It enters into the very fabric of the narrative. If, as Calvino states, "literature is a combinatorial game that pursues the possibilities implicit in its own material" then the rationale of this linguistic diversion becomes more than just an experiment in language for Rimanelli, as he suggests, but serves to show how this verbal communication is the origination of any disaccord between any two warring factions. To illustrate the importance and bipartisanship of the "word," it is during Benedetta's journey:

> The gun is a book, and the book is behind me, on the table, with a man dying on a stick. So one night I have a dream. Sweating and half-awake, I am aware of the book, still lying on the table, afraid of the dying man on the wooden stick. Sorrows are better. (80)

The book relates to the language of a society and, therefore, to its force and ferocity within this same culture. The significance of a single statement, according to Zip, is of very little importance. He adds that "Words are words, common property." (127) However, it is Joe, the guide for Benedetta, who states that he is "semantic" and, therefore, allows the reader to look beyond the simple story and delve into the linguistic game that the author has created by perceiving its grandness and its role, as demonstrated within this novel, by the clever use of proper names.

Although Capek Habekovic explains that Rimanelli's use of names within the text is amusing and, at the same time, attests to his break from cultural boundaries (212), his protagonist, from the books inception, states that she is "a former drag queen on the word stage" (33), suggesting her ability to alter her appearance as the need requires and the implicit and understated role that language plays. At a later point in the narrative Benedetta, actually, explains that her name is Clarence 'Benedetta' Ashfield. Here the linguistic teasing comes to a front position. Clarence could be a play on the American translation of the Italian word *chiarezza*. Moreover, the surname of the character, Ashfield, could suggest *i ceneri funebri*. Together the terms would refashion into the contradictory concept of transparent / sepulchral ashes. Her name Benedetta, also, could indicate that she is the "blessed" one, the hallowed voice of a generation that rings out clearly through the wickedness of the labyrinthine political struggle that has the populous lost in a quagmire of political language that perverts and corrupts the policy making within the American leadership. She is the Virgil that will guide the reader to understand the unpretentious, and yet powerful purpose of language. Benedetta is not a female or a person. She is an idea, a concept and, more importantly, her right to be heard echoes for all those young people who (although never heeded) opposed or died in an unprovoked and untenable war: Vietnam.

Additionally, Benedetta has had various "lovers," each appearing to play a part within the author's inventive use, and the ingenious role of language in a culture. The linguistic game evolves with its use within the political arena. Benedetta is constantly searching for the lexicon needed in order to tell her story, a saga of horror: the unwarranted war in Southeast Asia.

As a young girl, her first passion was for the teenager "Jargon," who she called Sandboy. According to Benedetta, Jargon was never able to totally enter her soul, although he was able to stimulate her for a limited time. His name, Sandboy, suggests the changeability of language, whereas Jargon refers to the use of slang in the contemporary world of discourse. Argot proves to be an ineffective power weapon against corruption, political or social, in a wartime culture. It is impotent in the rhetorical arena of government, precisely for its shifting and unstable values. Additionally, slang is not a suitable language to convince a culture to exit a war it cannot win.

Although there were several other lovers in the following few years, Benedetta's next major love interest was Willie "Holiday Inn" Sinclair. Again, the linguistic game comes to the foreground. The pronunciation of the name Willie could insinuate the expression "will he," allowing for the plausibility that the character *will or will not* be unequivocal in his selection of matters of state. The surname "Sinclair," moreover, could be a play on the Latin words, "Sine claritas," without clarity. The terms propose that the character could never be as comprehensible or as definitive as he could or should, and as a result, would not take an authoritative stand in a political battle. Willie, moreover, is the politician who speaks well but never says anything of substance. Precisely for his ambiguous posture, Zip has Willie eliminated. Although Benedetta apparently has a deep relationship with Willie, it is never consummated.[45] He states:

> The trouble with you is that you tease, and then you get scared and don't know how to go on when you see what you've done.
> He turned into a stern teacher, giving me advice and telling me about kneeing a guy when he goes too far, lifting his eyes. (125)

Zip the Thunder, as noted, is the Boss of all Bosses. He does not feel the necessity to explain himself or his actions. As the name evokes, he speeds through his work without ever studying the various components necessary to complete an action, its possible consequences or explaining the reasons for his making a decision. Zip

---

[45] "I fell into the rhythm of his body, and gave him my hand to let him teach me. But I still wouldn't let him suddenly break the branch" (124).

believes that his law, as the Executive Branch of the Commission, should be accepted without questions and without hesitation. He exiles Joe specifically because, Joe, the perennial student, wants to study all the facets of the family business and not accept blindly the word of one person. He, ultimately, kills Joe for his opposition to him. Moreover, Zip wants Benedetta to be his, although she rejects him. A union with her brings credence to his authority. Benedetta is the voice of a generation that opposes the war. Their unification, from Zip's perspective, alludes to a potential bond that could be created between the two opposing groups and should allow for the hostilities within the country to cease.

Finally, Benedetta's last love is Joe Adonis, the one person who stands up against the Administration and, specifically, against the overbearing and totalitarian power of Zip. His name comes from Hebrew and it is a specific reference to G-d. If, as Capek Habekovic states, Joe is the savior who comes down to Earth to save Zip and the band, and ultimately to save humanity from original sin (210), then his purpose is clear: to show the contemptible action that the Executive Branch of the government is pursuing in Vietnam, and to direct the country away from such a calamitous political path in which, until now, the voice of the people has been ignored.

His death at the end of the novel does not suspend his words. Benedetta is set free. She is pregnant with his child and as such will go out into the world and let them know that the war is wrong. The child is a new generation; a hope for a better future that allows the young to be heard and, more important, to take a political stand as the need arises.

The 1960s was an era of much political and social unrest: student revolts on major university campuses throughout the world; racial riots in major United States cities; technological advances that we are only now beginning to understand; and a war in another country that was causing a political and social revolution within the boundaries of the United States. It was a time of rapid and radical social change. The world in which Dante lived was similarly one of much political and social upheaval that ultimately had him exiled from Florence. Erich Auerbach has explained that it was the political tragedy and its affect through which Dante's destiny became consequential.[46] In his essay, "Dante and Florence," John M. Najemy points out that one of the poet's most memorable themes of the *Divina commedia* is his denunciation of the city of Florence. Dante, he added:

> excoriated the Florentines for the violence, factionalism, and instability of their politics, for their excessive pursuit and consumption of wealth, and, worst of all, for their criminal resistance to what he considered the divinely ordained authority of the Roman emperor.[47]

Here, in *Benedetta in Guysterland*, the political and social upheavals of the 60s are equally impressive and devastating for making Benedetta's fate meaningful. Giose Rimanelli's personal history of the devastation of the Italian Civil War plays an underlying basis for the reality in which he now finds himself: a nation on the verge of civil hostilities due to a schism that exists between the governing power and the people.

The Italian Civil War has played a huge role in the novels of this author and his horrific experiences within that brutal universe echo in many of his works. Relying on his rich medieval literary tradition and blending it with the existing contemporary actuality in his new

---

[46] Erich Auerbach, *Dante Alighieri: His Life and Works*, edited by Charles S. Singleton (New York: Harper and Row, 1965) 83.
[47] John M. Najemy, "Dante and Florence," in *The Cambridge Companion to Dante*, edited by Rachel Jacoff (Cambridge: Cambridge University Press, 1993) 80.

cultural environment, the author has created an avant-garde narrative that transcends time and geopolitics. *Benedetta in Guysterland* infiltrates the fabled and numinous world of betrayal. It shows that a society, any society, is responsible to all the people, at all times, and that no one person is above the law.

"She's Just a Devil Woman with Evil on Her Mind"
Giose Rimanelli's *Accademia*

I

Giose Rimanelli's second English language novel, *Accademia*,[1] appears, at times, to be a politically incorrect tale with an extremely disconcerting and negative image, creating a quasi stereotype figure, of women in the contemporary period. It is, notwithstanding, a narrative that, at first glance, appears to delve into the sexual mores of an enclosed universe, the University and its ivy-covered walls, by showing the interpersonal sexual relationships and dogmatic, childlike games of this, supposedly, sheltered community, and, at the same time, the insatiable quest for political power within the boundaries of this cosmos.

This novel is the second English language narrative of this Italian born writer, a trilogy of texts that the author initiates with *Benedetta in Guysterland*[2] and will, ultimately, conclude with his yet to be published manuscript *The Three-Legged One*.[3] The trio of narrations will encompass three distinct decades in the span of the author's creative life in his adopted new homeland, the United States, and, will cover three major influential and prejudicial conflicts of their respective times periods: Vietnam, equal rights movement, and the Watergate trials, each of which played an enormous and decisive role in the development of the social and cultural psyche of a nation. Rimanelli, already an established part of the world of Italian

---

[1] Giose Rimanelli, *Accademia* (Toronto: Guernica, 1997).
[2] Giose Rimanelli, *Benedetta in Guysterland* (Montreal: Guernica Press, 1993).
[3] Conversations with the author, March 2007.

letters of the post civil war years in the peninsula with his inaugural novel *Tiro al piccione*,[4] moves to the United States at the very start of the 1960s, a decade that he describes in his Italian anecdotal text, *Tragica America*, as "il decennio piú tormentato della storia dopo l'unificazione e il New Deal."[5]

In his first novel of this trilogy, *Benedetta in Guysterland*, the linguistic process penetrates the text, while undergoing an evolution that flourishes within each passing chapter, and ultimately presents a narrative that develops into a new genre, the liquid novel. *Benedetta in Guysterland*, like Rimanelli's first Italian narrative, *Tiro al piccione*, is an antiwar document that plays with the concept of time by shifting between two distinct eras: the Fascist period in Italy that brought the nation into a horrific civil war, and in the United States, the generational divide that existed during the Vietnam era, and thus produced a *quasi* civil war atmosphere. Like its predecessor, the game plan strategy of *Accademia* throws the reader immediately into a hastily moving and continuously altering maelstrom of a new crucial and confrontational era in American history that shaped another civil war-like ambiance in the nation: the Equal Rights Movement and the inflexible, closed-minded, authoritarian schism that it caused within the already combative nation during the Vietnam period:

> But that was a strange, Vietnamized, so to speak, epoch: The 1970s. Violence ran along a tightrope, and love was sparse and twisted, striking a precarious balance between morality and blasphemy. Often it was pure violence. And violence was as binding as love. There was much quarreling, and quarreling by no means precluded violence because it was already violence. The academics engaged in it with words

---

[4] Giose Rimanelli, *Tiro al piccione* (Milan: Mondadori, 1953 [Turin: Einaudi, 1991]).

[5] Giose Rimanelli, *Tragica America* (Genova: Immordino editore, 1968) 7.

knowing well that a word could be as destructive as the blow of a hand. Consequently violence, be it verbal or physical, invited vengeance.[6]

A new narrative, *Accademia* employs a hostile language combined with tinge silhouettes of mythical characteristics as weapons in its arsenal to create graphic images designed to illustrate the sociopolitical polarity of its contemporary period, the 1970s. These visceral images contrast with the various literary components of the author's rich artistic tradition, producing a *chiaroscuro* effect, reminiscent of the Italian Renaissance in order to introduce, within this narrative, a contemporary world in which a Dantean-like reality has now permeated the North American continent.

Coincidently, three years after the events of *Accademia* took place, in 1977, Rimanelli published his book *Graffiti*,[7] which, like this novel, presents a tale in which sexual politics plays a dominant role. In this experimental narrative, Rimanelli creates a unique and biting satire on the ever-altering character of women and the perpetual infernal in which men are bound to live if they refuse to accept this new view. In short, as men move into the twenty-first century, they are objurgated to damnation if they do not leave behind, rightly so in the past, their primitive concepts of women.[8]

With *Accademia*, the author presents a microcosm, the American University, steeped in an atmosphere of darkness and despair. The communal existence with all its consequences, quirkiness and intricacies play out in this narrative and govern the current time. To highlight the apprehensiveness and deprivation of trust that exists in the present era in his new communal atmosphere, Rimanelli tissues

---

[6] *Accademia* (15). All future references come from this edition.
[7] Giose Rimanelli, *Graffiti*, Titina Sardelli, ed. (Isernia: Editrice Marinelli, 1977).
[8] For more on this topic, see my *Crossing the Acheron: A Study of Nine Novels by Giose Rimanelli* (New York: Legas Publishing, 2000) 147-167.

within the current text corresponding situations of panic and fear that catapulted Europe and, specifically, the Italian peninsula, thirty years earlier, into its merciless infernal of the Civil War. Cognizant of his Italian medieval literary education, the author collimates this present-day historical period with the appalling world of the Fascist era that absorbed the peninsula from 1922-1945. The impetus, within the novel *Accademia*, for this constant clash between the two opposing social/gender groups, males and females, was a defining moment in American domestic policy that still persists today in the twenty-first century: the Equal Rights Movement. He then, carefully, juggles two dissimilar historical eras within two unlike universes at two extremely critical moments in their social and political developments.

In order for the author to engender the required binary passageway to usher us along through the social and political perdition of the 1970s, he must set in relief two specific time stages of analogous dismay: the European power struggle of the pre- and World War II years; and the 1970s, a period in which young women were now questioning more than ever their traditional social position in a world metamorphosing. Women were, now, resisting the blind acceptance of the erstwhile ways of a life forced upon them by others in their contemporary universe. They categorically rejected the ancient culture (ethnicity and background) and family (ancestors and kith and kin) values thrust upon them by an antiquated system of beliefs and thus created dismay not only in their male counterparts, but in earlier generations (males and females) who did not know how to adapt to this new ever changing world.

II

The basic story of *Accademia* is simple. A professor of social anthropology at Anabasis College in Nabokov County, Appalachia, and his wife are suffering a severe marital meltdown. The couple has been together for fourteen years. Simon Dona is an Italian born scholar, writer and documentary filmmaker from the region of Selimo. Lisa, his wife, is American from New Canaan, Connecticut, a graduate student in English literature, and the product of an illicit affair that her mother had with an Italian sailor prior to WWII. Through the course of Lisa and Simon's marriage they have been sporadically harassed by her mother and Lisa's perennial need to control the relationship with Simon by means of sentimental extortion. To escape the mother's firm grip on her daughter, Simon takes a position at a university in Canada on the opposite side of the North American continent. After a few years, Lisa demands to return to the United States. Simon then accepts a faculty position in California. In the meantime, Lisa, now pregnant, returns to her mother's house in New Canaan, Connecticut to give birth. She then leaves the new born child, a son, with her mother applying the rationalization that Simon and she must relocate to the States and that the baby, who could get lost in the upheaval, would be better taken care of by her mother. After various months and several efforts of persuasion by Simon, Lisa refuses to get the baby and, ultimately, threatens Simon with divorce if he continues to insist on her bringing the child back to live with them. Several years go by and, once again, Lisa wants to move, this time, geographically closer to her mother. Simon finds new employment at Anabasis College, not far from Lisa's mother's home (three hours), where their baby is being raised by the grandmother. Over the course of the next few years, the couple becomes friends with several members of the academic community. Eventually, Lisa finds out that Simon is having an affair with a younger female student and, then, in an attempt to continue her control of the marital relationship, begins to emotionally pressure her husband: first insisting, to Simon's mortification, on a ménage à trois with the very female student with whom Simon had the affair; and then proposing that she, too, would commence a sexual relationship with a man other than her spouse. Each suggestion causes more and more discord in their personal liaison. Ultimately, the couple divorce, and Simon finds himself, twenty years later, on another path in life, void of any pre-existing sentimental obstacles that may impede his journey and free to continue along a new route that may conduct him into a contemporary paradisiacal reality.

This, however, is not the first appearance of Simon Dona in a Rimanelli text. The same year in which *Accademia* appeared, 1997, the author also published his Italian novel *Detroit Blues*.[9] Yet, although the two novels with the same protagonist came out the same year, the chronological time period for both narrations is different. *Detroit Blues* takes place in the summer of 1967, during the race riots in the motor city; *Accademia*, on the other hand, although not specified, but easily calculated, is the year 1974, seven years after the former. Additionally, there is a slight variance in the name of the protagonist. In *Detroit Blues* his name is Simone Donato. In the seven years between the two time phases, his name has been Americanized. His wife's name, also remains constant, Lisa, and, as in *Accademia*, Simon is still a social anthropologist. At the same time, the presence of Lisa in the earlier time-frame novel is shadowy and, also intimates the impending marital problem that fully develops within this present narrative.[10]

---

[9] Giose Rimanelli, *Detroit Blues* (Welland, Ontario: Editions Soleil, 1977).

[10] "Ma a quel tempo, molto prima della tragedia, e lontano da Detroit ancora navigavi nella dolorosa e sadica ironia sessuale. In fondo punivi te stesso per i tuoi privati fallimenti: con Lisa ("Smettila de chiamarmi Bubala!") che non avresti dovuto sposare, ma che amavi perché c'era, esisteva; con la tua famiglia a Detroit che quasi mai vedevi e poco conoscevi, ma che amavi perché c'era, esisteva; con l'Italia e il seminario, il tuo *hortus* inconcluso, che non avresti mai dovuto lasciare: perché l'amavi, e non perché c'era. L'amavi perché ti aveva irrimediabilmente formato. Quello che eri prima sei ora" (54).

Detroit Blues, presented as a type of *romanzo giallo,* a mystery novel, has its protagonist, Simone, bearing witness to the social and racial hatred of the late 1960s. Now, in the 1970s, the same character attests to the gender wars, the battle of equal rights for women in the American University arena. Simon, therefore, is an attestant, although born in another country in which these polemics do not exist, to the social and political changes that are taking place in his new adoptive land and as such, has a fresh and open perspective of these impending transformations.

III

Rimanelli has declared that all his work is autobiographical in nature,[11] and that *Detroit Blues* is not an autobiography.[12] He does not operate, as George Gusdorf explains, as his own historian in this text.[13] There is no congruency between the narrator's voice, the writer's voice, and the protagonist. Nor is there, as Philippe Lejeune states, an autobiographical pact.[14] Rimanelli clearly states that:

---

[11] "My literature is almost all autobiographical in nature: novels, poetry, literary criticism. I date everything I write; on each completed work I mark down the hour, the day, the month and the year. And this is because I feel I am alone in the world. My writing, in fact, has never been directed at the world, rather, it reflects the reality of my own existence in direct contact with practical facts or ideals offered by my world's historical contingencies. My discourse, therefore, is more narrative than critical, more personal than objective. I learn by writing." (Giose Rimanelli, "Notes on Fascist/Antifascist Politics and Cultures from the Point of View of a Misfist," in *Rivista di Studi Italiani* 2 (Dec. 1984): 73.

[12] In her review of *Detroit Blues,* Roseanna Mueller states that *"Detroit Blues* hovers between history, autobiography, and novel" (*Italica* 75.3 (1998: 474). Also, Luigi Reina asserts "Trascorrendo tra autobiografia e storia..." (Book jacket, *Detroit Blues*).

13. George Gusdorf, "Conditions and Limits of Autobiography*,"* in *Autobiography,* James Olney, ed. (Princeton University Press: Princeton, 1980) 31.

14. Philippe Lejeune, *On Autobiography* (Minneapolis: University of Minnesota Press, 1989) 5.

> [...] *Detroit Blues* non è romanzo autobiografico... Potrebbe essere definito un'indagine al microscopio nelle segrete maglie dei gravi problemi sociali e razziali che nell'intimo delle coscienze umane e all'aperto travagliarono la città di Detroit in quell'epoca, e travagliano l'America tuttora. (206)

The author, to create the division between autobiography and fiction, uses a linguistic process of grammatical structures in order to concede a distancing, a detachment, between the narrator and the novelist. It plants the polemic between Rimanelli the *witness* of the tormented Fascist era in Italy during the pre- and Civil War years, and Simone, the *participant* in this mystery tale that recounts the senseless murder of his cousin while incorporating all the animus of the racial tensions of the period.

The variations between these two novels, although slight, appear to be in the use of the term *autobiography*. Rimanelli has clearly stated that *Detroit Blues* is not his own personal story. However, in this novel of parallels, *Accademia,* the presence of the author in the third part of the book is made even more poignant when he states:

> All I had done was to recount my personal history and that of another person dear to me, weaving a human and intellectual tapestry that I attributed to a husband, Simon, and to a wife, Lisa. Perhaps in order to distance myself from her? Perhaps to distance myself from myself? (170)

The line between autobiography and fiction becomes, therefore, blurred, contoured and intermingled within the text. The author, by doing so, sets in relief the peculiarity that exists between the two, totally different, genres. This idea coincides with that of Giovanni Cecchetti who, in his article "Autobiografia mitografica in Giose Rimanelli," states:

> Ciò che si può chiamare autobiografismo è in realtà qualcosa che si è trasformato in mito personale e che quindi sulla carta prende la forma di un mito. Lo scrivere, ripeto, può essere mitografia in senso molto generico, ma in fondo consiste in un riversare il mito fuori di sé e fermarlo, inchiodarlo sulla pagina, perché rimanga lì, per tutti, perché tutti lo possano vedere e tradurre in se stessi, nel loro mito personale.[15]

Rimanelli allows the reader the possibility of gleaning certain autobiographical elements from his novel without ever having a tangible role or actively participating within the storyline. It is his manner of a creative existence in order to play an objective role within the boundaries of an extremely subjective text, as is *Accademia*.

This objectivity allows for the differentiation of two distinct voices: one male, the other female, each showing, moreover, the correlation of time and the variations it creates within the framework of each character's personality. The immediate action of the two diaries encompasses a period of one week, seven days: the second week of August 1974. Time, in this text, is, like the novel itself, dichotomous and assists the reader in perceiving the binary pathway on which the protagonist journeys. Lisa, throughout her diary, identifies time as chronological, starting her entries with brief biographical moments of her earlier years and, finally, arriving to the present day. However, each of the former activities deals with factual items and takes a basic lineal approach to her life existence. Simon, on the other hand, has a fabulistic and ever evolving concept of diachronic moments that has him voyaging between the various time periods of his existence. These moments take him back to his native Selimo, in Italy, to re-experience his conflicted childhood, his lost adolescence when held as a prisoner in Villafranca during the country's civil war,

---

15. Giovanni Cecchetti, "Autobiografia mitografica in Giose Rimanelli," in *Rimanelliana*, Sebastiano Martelli, ed. (Stony Brook: *Forum Italicum,* 2000) 124.

and his first marriage to Sibyl, his Roman ex-wife. This intermingling of time frames grants the protagonist the facility to delve further into the present reality by shifting perspectives between the contemporary truth of the day and a long-ago lost optimism wounded from ageless and indefensible assaults:

> [...] and even time is no longer with me, she make me act. But time is a vague cognition; the writer finds it by isolating himself, the lover by exhibiting himself, by talking, by caressing. The best time is always that spent with another person; the worst is with a blank sheet of paper staring at you and the memory that fills it. It is a time-frame as narrow and vast as this house. (74)

The broad view of time, from the perspective of the protagonist, concedes for the accelerated transferring of historical instants between the universe that existed in Europe during the twenty years of the totalitarian dictatorship and the democratic American way of life that exists now during this critical era of social, political, and cultural metamorphosis, that seems to be, during this pivotal period, in a state of perpetual unbalance. Additionally, the view of time depicted by Simon licenses the blending of these two very dissimilar and culminating moments in the psyche of two disparate and yet, espoused people, Simon and Lisa, and, thereby, fostering the continuation of the dual environment established within the narrative.

Structurally, this novel consists of three parts, each recounted by a different voice. The first two parts of the narrative belong to the daily journals of the two main characters: Simon and Lisa. The third part of the tale, the *Appendix*, introduces the novelist, Giose Rimanelli, as a Pirandello-like character into the text. Each storyteller, moreover, has a specific number of chapters and each segment is congruent to the other: ten chapters per voice; thirty subdivisions in all. In the first segment, the narrator is Simon Dona and his part of the diary consists of ten chapters, although the tenth appears after the completion of his wife's entire account; the second, has the voice of his wife, Lisa, which has, like Simon, ten chapters; and the third part of *Accademia*, pertains to the novelist, Rimanelli, and coincidentally, ten chapters compose it. Moreover, Simon's chapters do not, apparently, follow a chronological design of discourse, as does Lisa's. His narration is a stream of consciousness that creates a puzzle-like pattern in which time is fragmented and not lineal. Each segment, like chess pieces, has a specific destination and, therefore, can stand independently from the other chapter or collectively to assist in the physical and emotional shaping of the entire story.

IV

In his novel *Benedetta in Guysterland,* Rimanelli suggests that he,[16] as writer, is taking a somewhat different path than the established, traditional map of literary development as explained by Vladimir Propp. In his *Morphology of the Folktale,* Propp purports that fairytales have limited fundamental theses and that these components are, for the most part, insistent in all narrative forms. He submits that all stories are, basically, variants of a single tale. They are patterned on determined structures and prefabricated elements all of which are placed in a multiplicity of combinations.[17] *Benedetta in Guysterland*, according to Rimanelli, hints that the archaic theories of storytelling are still present and prevalent in the contempo-

---

16. At one time in my life, as a master-builder-producer in another country I was sick with language and style. My body was covered with sentences, words, newspaper print. Then I took a shower. The tattoo's still showing, because I was not at all convinced that one can free himself at once of the inherited malaise Also because, following afro St. Augustine, I was constantly praying: "O G-d, send me purity and continence - but not yet." *Benedetta in Guysterland*, p. 28.

17. Vladamir Propp, *Morphology of the Folktale*, translated by Laurence Scott (Austin: University of Texas Press, 1979) 21-24.

rary, literary world. However, the author is endeavoring to liberate himself of this restricting literary tenet in which the language of the text provides the persona of the writer and, without leaving behind or contradicting his literary roots, is entering into a new stage in his creative triumph that permits the reader a considerable amount of interplay.

This idea, at the same time, echoes in *Accademia*. The author states that this novel was written twenty years prior to its publication and finds that, now in the present era, he has become, "partly, as Petrarch put it, 'a man other than what I am'" (155). This innovation reverberates the literary theory of Italo Calvino who explains that the writer survives within the act of composing and that authors must tear down and reassemble the process of literary composition.[18] Calvino, speaking of the function of literature, states:

> Literature is a combinatorial game that pursues the possibilities implicit in its own material, independent of the personality of the poet, but that it is a game that at a certain point is invested with an unexpected meaning, a meaning that is not patent on the linguistic plane on which we were working but has slipped in from another level, activating something that on that second level is of great concern to the author or his society. (22)

Rimanelli's *Benedetta in Guysterland* takes the traditional European novel, a formula that commenced *in illo tempore* with the storyteller, and changes it into a fresh American paradigm by redeveloping and rebuilding the shape and linguistic process of the story. He strips away the author from the narrative, for being excessive, and the text is, therefore, controlled by the reader who is being guided through the narrative by the language from within. The fable has,

---

18. Italo Calvino, "Cybernetics and Ghosts" in *The Uses of Literature*, translated by Patrick Creagh (San Diego: Harcourt Brace, 1982) 7-10.

therefore, been reinvented. A parallel scenario occurs, also, in *Accademia*. Twenty years after originally composing the story of Simon and Lisa, the author now reads the text as something else, something that occurred to another:

> In the hotel I re-read the manuscript. I realized that it was a novel in "autobiographical" form. I found myself outside it, as a writer, and inside it as a reader. I remembered some of those events vaguely; they were of a personal nature but the imaginary aspects - the language, for example - in effect had absorbed and distorted that which could be called reality. (170)

The writer, therefore, has successfully managed to disengage his reality from that of the narrative and, by doing so, has created a text that transcends the confines of traditional literary reality. Autobiographical elements have metamorphosed into mythical factors in which the universality of their existence take precedence over the personal realm of the writer.

At the same time, Rimanelli has re-created the physical formation of the frame narrative by purposely inverting the natural structure of this present day narration and having the outline of the story at the end of the text rather than at its installation. The palpable form of the tale is evocative, in a reversed and ironic manner, of Boccaccio's *Decameron* and, in such a way, creating a mystery style narrative of this novel, reminiscent of *Detroit Blues* in which Simon first appears. It is the end of the book that explains and clarifies the middle. More importantly, it is in the last segment, the *Appendix* in which the author presents himself and sets the stage for the entire text.

The structural architectonics of *Benedetta in Guysterland*, according to Romana Capek-Habekovic are rather traditional, although its extraneous components affirm little compatibility to its integral structure. She adds that in this first English novel of the author, Rimanelli deconstructs time, space, character and language leaving the interpreting of the narrative in the hands of lector and not the author.[19] It is, also, in this section of *Accademia* that Rimanelli notifies us, as he did previously in *Benedetta in Guysterland*, of a similar game plan strategy and his, again, invisible role within the volume by deconstructing the spatial and temporal elements of this narrative, thereby fashioning a modernist novel. Contrary to his earlier novels, the writer informs us that he has written a book in which:

> nothing is true in this manuscript. You have not liberated yourself from your personal history, you have invented another one by basing yourself on Jung. (159)

Rimanelli's presence, moreover, in this last division is, simultaneously, suggestive of Dioneo in the Florentine's work. He, alone, is given poetic license to speak about whatever he prefers, not being restrained to the events of the narrative and, in the end, informs the reader of the aftermath of the failed relationship between Simon and Lisa and his own personal and literary experiences in the twenty years since he originally composed the novel.

The irony comes to light when the author informs the reader that his manuscript was written by "Anonimo Selimano" (158), an obvious play on the name of Rimanelli's home region in Italy, Molise, and at the same time, an anagram for his regional connotation of being known as a "molisano." At the same time, the word "selimano" has no significance in the Italian language and, moreover, linguistically it produces a harsh sound and an awkward rhythm suggesting an alien element to this romance language. In a related

---

19. Romana Capek-Habekovic, "Texts Within the Text: Hermeneutics of the 'Fluid' Novel *Benedetta in Guysterland* for the Jabberwocky Reader," 208.

fashion, Rimanelli is proposing that this foreign component, like his protagonist, is a stranger within the boundaries of this new combative universe, the American academic world of the 1970s, and that this new reality is simulating all of the old ferocity and bitterness of the war years in the Italian peninsula.

Elements that appear within this final chapter resurface within the volume, as in the case of Boccaccio's work. Additionally, within the twenty chapters of Simon's and Lisa's story, there are tale bearing parentheses that deal with the book as a whole and that, at the same time, can stand autonomously from each other. As Boccaccio innovated the tale, presenting the archetypical storyline with its formalistic arrangement and language, Rimanelli's fable, on the other hand, inaugurates a fresh and stimulating postmodern structure in which time and space are altered to create a new post-modern realism, a massive jump forward carrying us into the future of literature.

Simon is now a professor in a small town called Appalachia. In *Benedetta in Guysterland*, this same small town is described as be ing primeval in demeanor and in language; words are superfluous, as "useless as speaking to a tree" (86). It is described as a *locus amenus* of Mid America in which the people seem to be modeled after the nature that surrounds them. Yet, paradoxically, much like the other protagonists' home area in the author's previous books, Appalachia is located in the mountainous regions of mid-America, while Molise, coincidentally, is in the central part of the Italian peninsula in the Matese mountain range. There is a resemblance of geographic features within the fabric of the author's former compositions and the present narrative. Furthermore, the description of lifestyles in this small rural community of the United States is interchangeable to the one that the author attributes to his home area in Italy. Appalachia, like Molise, is geographically separated, and distant, from all major cities thereby forming a world unto itself. Simultaneously, there is an exchangeable vibrancy, musicality and sonorousness between the names of the two locations: Appalachia and Appenninno.

V

Customarily, Molise has operated as the author's consecrated zone. According to Eliade, the sacred is equivalent to an unworldly power and to a divine reality.[20] In Rimanelli's novels of the 1950s, while the author's parents still resided in Italy, Molise functioned as this hallowed area. However, once the writer's family immigrated to America, first to Canada and then to the United States, Detroit eventually became the new sacrosanct domain. In addition, within the sacred space of Molise or Detroit, Rimanelli's parents' home constituted, that which Eliade further denominated as, the *axis mundi*, the center of the universe.[21] Profane space would, therefore, constitute anything that subsisted outside the chosen, consecrated area. In Rimanelli's novels, each time a character (Marco Laudato in *Tiro al piccione*; Nicola Vietri in *Peccato originale*; Massimo Niro in *Una posizione*) left the confines of his parents' home, the sacred space, the protagonist was confronted with the venomous and cruel realism of civil war, hatred, bigotry, and violence.

In *Detroit Blues*, the reader learns that Simon (nee Simone) was born in the coastal town of Termoli, in Molise. His parents, ultimately, move to Detroit just at the start of the hostilities in Europe (1939). Now, in *Accademia*, Simon explains that his mother was Québécois, although in *Detroit Blues* she is from the United States. Both mothers, however, were born in North America and transported at an early age to reside in Molise, and each was insistent that

---

[20] Mircea Eliade, *The Sacred and The Profane*, translated by Willard R. Trask (San Diego: Harcourt Brace, 1959) 12.
[21] Mircea Eliade, *Images and Symbols: Studies in Religious Symbolism* (New York: Sheed and Ward, 1969) 39.

her son receives a conservative religious education that was, eventually, rejected by him. At the same time, Simon relates in *Accademia* that he fought in Italy's civil war, on the wrong side, and that he was a prisoner of the Fascists in Villafranca, although in *Detroit Blues* he submits that he spent the war years cloistered in a religious seminary, away from the horrific brutality that a war manifests, only to have to fight to protect himself from the ferocious social and cultural whims of the young seminarians and the clerical instructors. These deviations, nonetheless, do not alter the relationship between the protagonists of both novels.

Simone's parents' house in Detroit, in *Detroit Blues,* serves as the center of his world. However, by late 1997 when this book was published, Rimanelli's parents had passed away and there no longer existed, as in the past, a personal link with Molise or Detroit.[22] The lack of this concrete connection would necessitate, by definition, the inversion of Molise into Selimo; the bond, albeit physically broken, is still emotionally attached.

A divergent element, therefore, enters into *Accademia* not witnessed in any of Rimanelli's Italian books. The protagonist declares that he is, now, not from Molise, but the fictitious region of Selimo, the anagram of this central area of Italy. By inverting the letters of his home region, the author appears to distance himself from it, however he is, actually, protecting it, cocooning it, within his quintessence. Furthermore, this reversal of the spelling of a geographic area esteemed to the writer could also suggest the significant move from one continent to another, each on an opposite side of the ocean, and by this means, establishing a transposition of his previous existence. At the same time, the name Selimo evokes the poem *La ballata di Joe Sèlimo,* by this author in his book *Moliseide,*:

---

[22] Vincenzo Rimanelli died on August 8, 1988; Concettina Rimanelli passed away on October 13, 1996.

"Devil Woman with Evil on Her Mind"

> Sono chiuso in una stanza
> piccolina come il mondo.
> Rido e danzo, a volte piango,
> sono intenso come il mondo.
> Alla fine, rassegnato
> ho sposato l'emozione.[23]

In his introduction, Luigi Bonaffini explains that Rimanelli perceives himself with the character Joe Sèlimo and that the epic is a state of mind that connotes compenetration of actual visualizations in the illusory framework of imaginativeness (xix). Rimanelli hints at the sanctity of a small, enclosed space offered to his persona by comparing it to the world at large. Within its limited, geographic boundaries, Joe is able to journey across time and space, thereby attesting to their intermingling and the harmonious blending between these two distinct concepts. This is an idea that runs parallel in Rimanelli's current literary work and is brought to light by the author's specific use of his new sacred center: a room, *una stanza.*

In *Accademia,* the sacred space manifests itself in the house in which Simon and Lisa reside in Appalachia. It is an abode, made of glass, in which their daily events come to light, and like the elements from which it is made, the house will show itself to be fragile, as is the relationship between these two people. In this dwelling the reader becomes aware of the entire personal history of the two characters: Simon's existence prior to his arrival in the United States; his relationship with Lisa from its inception to the present day; Lisa's mother and her long ago illicit affair that produced her; the dominance of this mother over her child; Simon's professional obligations; Lisa's erotic dreams; the various comings and goings of pro-

---

[23] Giose Rimanelli, "Ballata di Joe Sèlimo" in *Moliseide: Songs and Ballads in the Molisan Dialect,* translated by Luigi Bonaffini (New York: Peter Lang, 1992) 48.

fessional and artistic friends who enter and leave this house at will; and finally, the extramarital affair that, ultimately, appears to cause the end of their marriage. Within the boundaries of this consecrated area, their family house, there functions an *axis mundi* within this confined reality: the small glass room they call Pearl Gate. The name of this room indicates its absolute sanctity in that it reminds the reader of the words of *Revelation 21:21*:

> And the twelve gates were twelve pearls: every several gate was of one pearl: and the street of the city was pure gold, as it were transparent glass.

According to the New Testament, there were twelve gates that led to the entrance of the heavenly city of Jerusalem. Each is named for one of the twelve tribes of Israel and an angel is positioned next to each gate. Additionally, each of the gates is made of pearl, an object made from the suffering of the oyster. Once the voyager is inside the sacred walls of Jerusalem, the problems of life that they endured, their suffering, will now cease and lead to a beautiful place. It is at this moment that the voyage into heaven is determined.

If as Eliade states the *axis mundi* is the very center of the world, the area in which all three cosmic levels (earth, heaven, hell) unite (1959, 36), then this room in Simon and Lisa's house function as its sanctified center. It is in this space that Simon and Lisa engage in afternoon lovemaking. It is where Judy Madison, a colleague of Simon's and friend of Lisa's, insisted on spending a night, rather than returning to her home nearby or staying in the guest cottage when Lisa was out of town. It is, also, the place in which Lisa, for the first time, encountered Simon making love to another female, Rose, and ultimately, it is the spot from which their marriage totally disintegrates. Pearl Gate, the sacred center of their universe, the portal that should initiate their voyage into paradise, ironically and poignantly sets them on a different path that carries them on a journey to the bowels of hell.

All space, therefore, that pertains to the world outside this sanctified zone would have to, then, constitute a profane universe. Each time a character of Rimanelli's enters into this unsanctified area, he is confronted with the horrors of civil unrest. In this novel, ironically, the corrupt area of Simon's life is the University, a place that should offer constant solace and the unending search for pure knowledge. Instead, this institute of higher education becomes a hotbed for political insecurities of the time. In this unholy area he is confronted by the socio-politics of the academic world in which knowledge is not sufficient for advancement, but rather social and cultural connections play a paramount role.

VI

Rimanelli's novels of the 1950s, a ten-year period that the author identifies as "his time,"[24] deal with man's maltreatment of force and its ensuing effects in a political, social, economic, and cultural post war-torn Italy. They operate as a base to and an indication of the anecdotal process and development that expand within this English novel for this Italian-born narrator. *Accademia*, like its Italian literary precursors by Rimanelli, grapples with the exploitation of individual domination over man's fear and loathing of a competing social group, now, however, in a new era and in a new geographic location. The geopolitics of the era has transformed, taking on the battle cry of the war between the genders. In Rimanelli's tale the perversion is shown to exist, as in his earlier Italian narratives, within the political, communal, fiscal, and enlightening realms of the modern era, the 1970s; and it becomes apparent by the cultural-political

---

[24] Conversations with the author, the most recent, 18 April 2006.

conflict that takes place in the United States University system due to the failure of the American populace to accept the Equal Rights amendment.

During the 1950s, Rimanelli produced, in a period of less than ten years, five books: *Tiro al piccione*; *Peccato originale*; *Biglietto di terza*; *Una posizione sociale*; and *Il mestiere del furbo*.[25] Each of these tales, narrated in a traditional format, treat the socioeconomic and political subjugation of the age that its characters abide while exhibiting, simultaneously, their Orphic journey through the heinous days of their existence in a universe that imparts very little hope of salvation. *Tiro al piccione,* Rimanelli's first book, tenders the reader the story of an immature boy who fights on the wrong side of the Italian Civil War and who witnesses man's ill-treatment of his fellow human in a fratricidal ceremony that plays out *illo tempore*; *Peccato originale* handles the penury of a post civil war period in which the inhabitants of a small, southern village must emigrate to the New World because of their powerlessness to advance, fiscally and socially, in a closed surroundings; *Biglietto di terza* depicts the backbreaking existence of the immigrant, from his embarkation in the Old World, to his collective and financial establishment in the New World; *Una posizione sociale* portrays the social inequalities that exist in Italy during the prewar years by comparing it to the post civil war years in the United States; and *Il mestiere del furbo* tackles the ill-usage of power within the confines of the literary and artistic world.

Additionally, correlations can be made between *Accademia* and Rimanelli's other narratives of the 1950s. The civil war years in which Simon blindly ends up fighting on the wrong side is directly related to *Tiro al piccione*; the postwar period in which he roams the world

---

[25] *Tiro al piccione* (Milan: Mondadori, 1953), *Peccato originale* (Milan: Mondadori, 1954), *Biglietto di terza* (Milan: Mondadori, 1958), *Una posizione sociale* (Florence: Vallechi, 1959), *Il mestiere del furbo* (Milan: Sugar, 1959).

in search of a meaningful existence, ultimately, becoming a scientist could be associated to *Peccato originale*; his arrival in the United States in order to embark on a new life reminds the reader of *Biglietto di terza*; his parents desire for the young boy to get an education prompts us to consider *Una posizione sociale*; and the negative behavior of female colleagues, playing power and manipulative games, in the cultured world of American academia is shown to be at the heart of *Mestiere del furbo*.

The temporal repositioning occurs one evening in which Simon reads a letter from his friend from Italy, Ugo. His compatriot tells him about the political debacles occurring in Italy, and compares it to an outlandish farce that amuses the populace. At the same time, Ugo is concerned that the aftermath of this fiasco will plunge the country into a deeper cultural quagmire, allowing for terrorism to take a foothold in the peninsula. At the conclusion of his letter, Ugo asks him about his life in Appalachia. While contemplating the correspondence Simon refers to Lisa being absent, in New York with her mother, and that with her out of town, he is left remembering his entire life:

> I feel her absence and desire her presence. I get drunk and get mixed up. The phone rings now and then, and finally all that remains is the blank sheet staring me in the face. I am a Xenophon, yes, trying to write my very private *Anabasis*. Remembrance is the only presence, along with sleep. (74)

Here, within the specificity of the text, the impending journey of Simon is imminent, and, simultaneously, it sets the stage for the repositing of temporal realities within the framework of his sanctified area of the house. His trek will take him back to his childhood days in Selimo, through the nightmarish realities of Italy's civil war, to the postwar years when he was in search of his career, his failed marriage to Sibyl, his introduction into American academia, and finally, to his present day existence in Anabasis.

The name of this institute of higher education in which he is a professor is Anabasis College and it prompts the reader, as Simon observes, of the classic work of Greek literature by Xenophon. Despite the fact that the saga recounts the chronicle of a large Greek army of 10,000 mercenaries employed by Cyrus the Younger to capture, from his brother Artaxerex II, the throne of Persia, the term itself has come to pertain to a long journey.

Classic literature has, according to Rimanelli, been a font of his literary experience. In the preface to his book *Moliseide*, a compendium of 100 poems written in his native Molisan dialect and in Italian, the author states, regarding this collection of poetry, that:

> If the *Aeneid* sings the glory, we sing our everyday passions: love, pain, anger, the quarrel, the reconciliation, the dirty trick, the distant land, dreams, desires, ghost - and not to make immortal art as Virgil did (almost impossible nowadays, times being what they are, and ironically given the label of *post-modernism*) but pop-pap. Even with this the memory of your roots can be saved. (xix)

Bonaffini further clarifies that in *Moliseide*, a book that the author delineates as an epic journey, Rimanelli has the obsession to return to literary origins that are bound up with his cultural background (xxvii).

Nevertheless, in *Accademia*, the author takes classic European literature and threads it with the sexual revolution culture of a generation, specifically the concept of open marriage and its lack of conjugal restrictions imposed by earlier generations, and creates a post-modern labyrinthine reality in which this new political morality takes the reader on a journey through the realms of a new civil conflict in American life: the role of women in contemporary society and the unending cultural and social struggles that take place between two distinct segments of the populace, men and women.

To highlight the absurdity of conflict and war, the author, at the very start of this novel, creates a narrative situation that parallels the story of Cain and Abel by introducing the children from two different wives and who have two distinct cultures: one American and the other Italian. Here, Simon is reminiscing about the pseudo relationship that exists between his sons; two, Sandro and Dino, are the product of his marriage to Sibyl, his Roman ex-wife; and the third, Daniel, is from his union with Lisa. The three do not truly know each other and there is an innate animosity in Sandro toward Daniel:

> [...] This so-called brother is actually a stranger as was Sandro for that matter, whose acquaintance he had made only last summer. Nor has Daniel forgotten Sandro, his father's eldest son, a youngster savage and malign, a sly *provocateur*, who sported a scornful mustache in the manner of a West Point cadet. In Sandro's eyes Daniel "the kid" was a fat pinkish piglet to be roasted on a spit. Through him Lisa intuits Sibyl's revenge, Sibyl the Roman lady whose man had walked off on her wantonly and capriciously, subsequently dubbing divorce love.
>
> One day Daniel fell in the canal on Cape Cod, his first real terror of his life. He was drowning in the water under the eyes of this guffawing strange who watched him from the bridge. (8)

Sandro, like Cain, only wants to see the demise of his half-brother. His jealousy towards his younger sibling is uncontrollable and malicious. More importantly, Cain's reaction to his brother was of a political nature: the social politics of the family. He sees Abel as a threat to his place within the family unit and to gain superiority over his brother, he must kill him. Obliterating Abel would place Cain, from his standpoint, in a higher realm of esteem. His offering to G-d is, notwithstanding, of a considerably less value than that of Abel's because it is not sincere. His failure is not to see that the action of fratricide would place him in a contemptible relationship with the Almighty. In a similar manner, the extinction of Sandro's sibling would, by his definition, remove any obstacle between him and his father and put him in a posture of greater importance. The existence of Daniel, moreover, suggests to Sandro that this child of another woman is the only reason for which the father abandoned the mother and, consequently, forsaken his Roman children. From Sandro's perspective, therefore, the elimination of Daniel would propose the eradication of the marriage of Simon and Lisa and, in the final analysis, Simon's return to his former life with his brother, Dino, and their mother, Sibyl. Sandro, like Cain, is unable to comprehend that Daniel is not his enemy. Simon's relationship with Lisa had nothing to do with his Roman children and his new life in America. Sandro, therefore, has created a division in Simon's world: Italy and the United States; his Roman children and his American child, and in such a way, he is establishing an erroneous barrier between two nonexistent distinct worlds. Simon does not recognize a divergence between these two spheres; they, his children, are all equal in his eyes, and from his perspective, only one universe exits, and the politics of the family is absent and imaginary. Sandro's behavior, therefore, like Cain's would only cause contempt in the eyes of his father.

René Girard explains that physical vehemence can be a consecrated act. He states; "violence is the heart and soul of the sacred."[26] Girard points out that killing without sacrifice is the fundamental inviolable act because it is the reincarnation of the Cain and Abel's story; the holiness rests in that the sacrificial victim is forgotten and replaced by a surrogate victim (5). Abel, the shepherd, had an offer-

---

[26] René Girard, *Violence and the Sacred*, translated by Patrick Gregory (Baltimore: The John Hopkins University Press, 1989) 31.

ing to give to G-d; Cain, the farmer, did not. Cain executed his brother in anger.[27] Therefore if, as Girard points out, brutality were a hallowed act, then war—civil war—would be an action that transports man back *illo tempore*.

Mircea Eliade, additionally, states that a myth connects a sacred history, a primal occurrence that took place *ab initio*. The allegory is history that took place, *in illo tempore*. Once told, the enigma becomes an unconditional legitimate action; it constitutes a validity that is unequivocal.[28] If, however, as Eliade states, myth is always the recital of a creation and it speaks only of realities, then the myth that Rimanelli is trying to uncover is the brutality and foolishness of civil hostilities.

VII

The author's personal history of his involvement in Italy's Civil War is not restricted to his first book, *Tiro al piccione*. It is a tragic saga that goes beyond this archetypal narration and is echoed in many of the Rimanelli's stories including *Graffiti, Il tempo nascosto tra le righe*,[29] in which Marco Laudato, the protagonist of *Tiro al piccione*, re-appears in the contemporary era, *Familia, Il viaggio*,[30] *Benedetta in Guysterland* and now, in *Accademia*. Each of these novels carries the reader back and forth between two very separate epochs: the contemporary period in America and the war years in Europe. All of these texts bring to light the social and political agitation of a nation during various periods of social and civil unrest.

An intertextual element within this narrative that highlights the civil animosity between the sexes is the relationship that exists be-

---

[27] *Genesis* 4:1-9.
[28] *The Sacred and The Profane*, 95.
[29] Giose Rimanelli, *Il tempo nascosto tra le righe* (Isernia: Marinelli Editore, 1986).
[30] Giose Rimanelli, *Il viaggio* (Isernia: Iannone, 2003).

tween Simon and his mother-in-law Cress, an affluent and domineering American woman. This diminutive name provokes the reader to recall the classic medieval narrative poem of Boccaccio, *Il filostrato*. According to the Florentine's story, the narrative poem has a mythological plot in that it recounts the story of Troilo, a younger son of Priam of Troy, and Criseida, daughter of Calcas. Calcas, a Trojan prophet, foresaw the surrender of the city and, therefore, joined the Greeks, abandoning his daughter in Troy. Troilo gains Criseda's love with the assistance of his friend Pándaro, who is Criseida's cousin. She swears eternal love for Troilo. Nevertheless, in a consequent exchange of captives, Criseida is sent away to the Greek camp at her father's request. The Greek hero Diomedes falls in love with her and succeeds in seducing her. Troilo learns of his lover's betrayal when the Trojan Deífobo returns to the city with the clothes that he has seized in battle from Diomedes. On these gowns is a brooch that belonged to Criseida. Troilo, enraged, goes into combat to search out Diomedes. Although he is able to cause harm among the Greek ranks, he does not find Diomedes, and is, finally, slain by Achilles. Most importantly, however, is that the story centers on the emotional consequence on Troilo of detachment from his beloved, and his desperation when he discovers Criseida's betrayal.

In Rimanelli's narrative, there is an ironic twist to the original story with the tale of Simon's mother-in-law, Cress, and her behavior towards him. Although married to a French teacher, she had a long time relationship with an Italian sailor. This amorous affair produced Lisa. At the start of World War II, the sailor died in combat. Lisa is raised, extremely protectively by the mother (who never leaves her side, even while sleeping) until she attends college, where Lisa meets and falls in love with Simon. Cress views Simon as the reincarnation of the lover she lost and does everything possible to break their marital relationship so that she could have a physical involvement with him. She, furthermore, believes that Simon is the rebirth of her dead Genovese lover, who came back to retrieve Lisa so as to reconcile her to sepulchral old age and shriveled up widowhood.[31] Cress is willing to betray her daughter, without consideration of the dreadful consequences, for a possible bond with Simon. Parallel to the Boccaccio story, Cress believes she was given up by her lover and takes another Italian partner with whom she has a relationship for over 35 years. She, like Troilo, perceives an abandonment from her former amorous mate and, as such, the appearance of Simon in the life of Lisa, reminds her of her first love and she now feels the need to punish. Simon, on the other hand, wants nothing to do with Cress and moves across the continent with Lisa to escape the grasp of this woman.

Boccaccio's setting of the story of Troilo and Criseida is Trojan, however, it is not a tale from Greek mythology, but from the twelfth-century French medieval re-elaboration of the Trojan legend by Benoît de Sainte-Maure, known to Boccaccio, in the Latin prose version, by Guido delle Colonne. Yet, the mother-daughter relation between Cress and Lisa is most closely evocative of the Greek myth of Demeter and Persephone. Like Demeter who believes that her daughter was stolen from her and taken to the underworld by her Uncle, Hades, against her will, Cress will do anything to get her daughter away from this person she deems socially unworthy and have her returned to their home far away from this individual.

At the same time, Lisa giving her child, the baby Daniel, to her

---

[31] In Lisa's diary she states: "I believe that Cress, jealous and displeased, must have been wrecked form many nights and days by the crazy notion that the stranger Simon was none other than her Italian lover who had died at sea at the outbreak of World War II. And that now, transformed, he had come back to her in the guise of Simon in order to retrieve his daughter by marrying her and relegating Cress to unsmiling old age and withered widowhood." (83)

mother to raise and nurture is reminiscent of the biblical passage of Moses and the story of Exodus in the *Old Testament*. According to Judaic belief, the Pharaoh of Egypt had condemned all sons of the Hebrews to be put to death. Yocheved, the mother of Moses, desperate to prolong his life, floats him in a basket down the Nile. Pharaoh's daughter, hearing the cries of the baby as she walks by, pities the child and adopts him as her own.[32] In a barbed manner, a variation of the same story is presented within this text in that Cress has threatened and harassed Simon throughout his relationship with Lisa, but never the son. Lisa, in order to free herself of all responsibility regarding this child and to extend her relationship with Simon, surrenders him willingly, and against Simon's will, to be nurtured by her mother. Yocheved thought only of the safety and life of her child and was, as a result, totally selfless in her actions; Lisa, contrarily, only considered herself, and as such, manifests as a selfish person.

Simon, like the Israelites escaping the wrath of the Egyptians, moves across the continent to find a better life, only to encounter that Lisa sacrifices their child to a "false" mother. Ironically, also, is the fact that Lisa deposited her child, Daniel, with her mother in the town of New Canaan, Connecticut, a place that should be the parallel of the biblical promised land of "milk and honey" assured to the Jews fleeing captivity. New Canaan however, in Simon's saga, is a location that attests to the bondage Lisa's mother has over her and produces an isomeric image of the real heaven. Simon's journey, therefore, into the "real" Canaan, like the Israelites, will be postponed because of Lisa's idolatrous actions; she refuses to abandon the intimate thrall she has towards her mother. Simon, moreover, a name that corresponds to one of the twelve tribes of Israel, Simeon,

---

[32] *Exodus* 2: 1-10.

"Devil Woman with Evil on Her Mind"

is still in search of a homeland. However, this tribe of Israel, like one of the ten lost tribes, finds itself now irretrievable within the political quagmire of an academic community. Additionally, the name Simon could suggest a derivation of the Hebrew word Sh'mah, the central tenet of Judaism. It is with these six words that the Jewish people, who recite it four times a day, announce their belief in a monotheistic message in which there is only one G-d. These few words separate the Jewish people from the idolaters who worship false and multiple gods. Lisa, who appears to worship a false god in the figure of her overbearing mother, is condemned not to enter the promised land of Canaan and consequently is dispatched only as far as the limits of the pseudo/ false New Canaan. Simon, on the other hand, will have to, ultimately, make the journey by himself.

Simon's transcendental voyage through the various time periods of his life coincides the day in which Lisa has gone to New York City to spend the day with her mother. As he is reading the correspondence from Ugo, he realizes that sleep is an escape from the loneliness he suffers with Lisa away:

> I sleep more than ever when she's not here, weariness accumulates and sleep shakes it off. I gently indulge in ironic self-reflection, observing my face in profile. (74)

The journey that the protagonist makes, is in a type of hypnogogic state, and is one that agrees with Eliade's concept of *dream time*: a return to the start, *ab initio*, of creation; man must re-create the myth, *illo tempore*, of his own beginnings (*imago mundi*). *Dream time* empowers man to reincorporate the sacred time of the commencement of things, and, therefore, to renew the world.[33]

---

[33] Mircea Eliade, *Rites and Symbols of Initiation*, translated from the French by Willard R. Trask (New York: Harper Torchbooks, 1958) 6.

The hostility that Simon encounters is not limited to his Roman son, Sandro, but also extends to his wife's mother, Cress. Simon is, therefore, the victim of hostility from two very distinct cultures: Italian / American; male / female, each assume anger and ferocity within the family unit, thereby tearing it apart bit by bit. Simon's diary narrates the story of fratricide (Cain and Abel) and familial betrayal (Demeter and Persephone) and it carries the reader *ab initio*, simultaneously, allowing the reader to perceive the civil hostilities he now faces in a new dynamic of the United States in the 1970s. *Accademia*, like its predecessors, illuminates a civil war like ambiance that existed between men and women in the United States work environment by pinpointing the gender aggression that permeated the university campus: male and female faculty.

VIII

Chronological time repositioning occurs, one evening, in which several of the colleagues and friends of Lisa and Simon gather to view his new documentary, *The Twelfth Macaque*. Simon and another colleague, Andrew, decided to create a film based on some of the prevailing sexual theories of the day, without taking a personal stance on the issue: "that man can be divided into *one-animal* men and *two-animal* men." (13) The purpose, notwithstanding, of the film was to entertain and elicit reactions from their coworkers at the university. However, a debate ensued and reactions were divided between genders. The male perspective of the documentary was that females animals, specifically, the seagull, tended to be homosexual in nature, whereas the male seagull showed no tendency to this behavior. One male faculty member contrived a seminar on the topic that the females understood as being discriminating towards their role in academia. Neither of the filmmakers had a specific vision of the work. Simon, although hesitant to discuss his opinion on the sexuality of the seagull, ultimately when pushed, stated that he believed that the female of the species was neither essential nor committed, and therefore, he, too, was now looked upon with suspicion from the females there.

At the same time, Simon points out, the evening in which the view the film, that:

> I have always been enamored of clouds. One of them, Judy Madison, crouches herself on my head and carries me off. I'm alone. I'm perfectly alone. Yet memory continues to make something of the past surface to consciousness, and offers me the continuity of time. (38)

This idea runs parallel to that of Micea Eliade's of cosmic time. According to Eliade, the religious man in general, the archaic, lives in a recurrent present. He repeats the signs of another and, through this reiteration, lives always in an atemporal present.[34] History is, as Vico proclaims, cyclical in nature, and in the case of Simon, his Orphic journey is about to repeat itself for the third time.

The horrific past that Simon experienced during the war years in Italy, begin to reappear the evening in which he shows his documentary and the reactions it generates with the spectators. The film elicited two very distinct political reactions, along the lines of gender, each on opposite sides of the spectrum. Men perceived the theme of betrayal and the story of Judas, while women saw a "comic operetta on hedonism" (43), believing that the biblical subtleties were perceptible and, at the same time, relegated the female to a subordinate role. The dichotomous perspective of the audience sets the stage for the imminent battle and it is through this labyrinth of symbols and signs that Simon will need to navigate in order to survive.

---

[34] Mircea Eliade, *The Myth of the Eternal Return*, translated from the French by Willard R. Trask (Princeton: Princeton University Press, 1974) 86.

The watchful lector of the novels of Rimanelli is sharply aware of the genuineness in each of these aforementioned narratives and perceives their presence, blended and integrated, punctuated within this new fable of *Accademia*. The atrocities of the Italian Civil War that Marco Laudato suffers in *Tiro al piccione* are reverberated within this new text. Italian Fascism, and its oppressive form of governance, explain Simon's unenviable participation, and ultimately, forced imprisonment in Villafranca, in a war in which he did not want to participate. At the same time, there is the presence of another character, Matthias Freedman, a professor of comparative endocrinology, whose family was eliminated in the Nazi death camps. Abuse and barbarity were not limited in this novel to Italy but encompassed the whole of Europe during a period in which, as Matthias Freedman explains; "the life of cockroaches was better than that of prisoners in the hands of the Nazis" (18).

More importantly, Matthias Freedman is, at present in Anabasis College, its Vice President. As a child, after the war, he served as a witness at the Nuremberg Trials of 1945-1946 in order to bring to justice the Nazi instigators who had killed his parents in the camps of Dachau. Now, in the current time, he has determined to retire from the academic world due to a similar political upheaval:

> "I'm handing in my resignation from this place next year," added Matthias. "There's altogether too much politics on the one hand, and altogether too much wordly-minded activity, on the other. We're all losing our tempers, all of us ... Do you really want to stay on here?" (68)

As the surname of this character suggests, Freedman, Matthias liberated himself from the horrors of the Nazi atrocities by attending and participating in the trials of the crimes against humanity, and now he is, once again, emancipating himself from the political ferocity infusing itself within the university confines. He recognizes that it is language that is corrupting the free interchange of ideas within the academic world, as it was the specific language of 30 years earlier that caused the creation of the German death camps by insisting that they were actually work camps. Moreover, the captured Nazi's at the Nuremberg Trials, in an attempt to exonerate their horrific actions of the war years, employed political and social word games as the justification for their barbaric activities, relying on linguistic game plan patterns to change and revise the history of an era.

To illuminate the other side of the spectrum of academic life, there is a character by the name of Charlotte Shark, a name that arouses all the fierceness and vehemence of the ocean by depicting a creature that is dangerous and deadly to man. Charlotte, a professor of linguistics, is a member of the academic Inner Circle in which political potency was centered. She is the counterweight to Matthias Freedman. Both Matthias and Charlotte, administrators in the governance of the campus (one male, the other female) insisted on scholarship and teaching for all in the academic community. However, from Charlotte's perspective, although the men weren't much more prepared than the female, they had more job experience behind them and their peer reviewed evaluations were always at a higher level. She believed that this suggested that the female professor's publications were scarce and, simultaneously, of an inferior quality, and therefore, the female was judged more severely than the male. Most importantly, however, is her physical and psychological description:

> [...] had a nice appearance, but she eternally dressed as a male and wore half-length boots. She was athletic, her laughter was frank, her speech proper, and she gave the impression of having been a voracious reader. The truth of the matter, however, was only one: She was power-mad and vindictive to the point of hysteria. (41)

"Devil Woman with Evil on Her Mind"

The physical appearance of this woman is one that brings to mind the Nazi Storm Troopers with their black leather boots and athletic framed bodies. At the same time, her emotional description parallels that of the authoritarian power hungry Fascist of the first half of the 20th century when hate and bigotry controlled the politics of the day.

Language, to Charlotte, is something that can be manipulated and bent so as to depict a negative attribute even when one is not present. Charlotte is the person who convinces Lisa that, upon finding out that Simon had a physical relationship with a student, she should seek an attorney. At the same time, Charlotte, taking the personal problems of this married couple, uses the information with the hopes of getting Simon dismissed from the institute. Professional and personal activities are not separated, but used as ammunition to destroy a person's life.

Freedman survived the Nazi horrors to be able to attest to the German religious hatred of the war years and Shark is the person who is now attempting, politically, to bring the university back to a ghetto-like existence in which there is a separation and differentiation between the male and female faculty that is producing an odious atmosphere. Her speech pattern, therefore, is one that not only creates an abominable social environment in which the colleagues must work but, at the same time, is aggressively and maliciously incriminating all males of certain behavioral traits that infect the political domain of the college.[35]

In archaic communities, according to Eliade, young men must pass a rite of initiation in which the first stage of this procedure is the

---

[35] "Charlotte felt outraged by the male world. From her observation post in the Inner Circle she persistently pointed out to various deans and vice-presidents how necessary it was to reevaluate the position and the status of women in civil service jobs, particularly when they are academics" (104).

detachment of the catechumen from his mother. This severance, sometimes violent, is a split with the world of childhood; the novice essentially embarks upon the sacred universe of adulthood. The revelation of the reverent means that the young man, in a short amount of time, understands the whole body of his cultures' mythological and humanizing customs. Furthermore, the passage from the profane world to the sacred suggests an experience of death: the destruction of one life for another. If, as Eliade states, the maternal universe is the profane world, then breaking away from it, even demolishing it, would be a sacred act (3-9).

The initiation rite would have to bring the apprentice into the sacred world of human sacrifice, the act that transports him back *ab initio* and, eventually, to the re-enactment of the myth of Cain and Abel, epitomized, in contemporary society, by civil war. Simon sees the college as a mother figure:

> The College was the mother to whom we attributed guilt and wonder, death and metaphor, hope and judgment, faith and malice, and sentimentalism to boot. The result was that today the reaction is harsh and uncompromising. (15)

He perceives the academic universe as a matriarchal consistency; nurturing, supportive and protective of all its members within the enclosed walls of the institute while, apparently, shielding them from the corrupt world that exists beyond its boundaries. He has been an academic, according to his calculations, for nearly fourteen years, starting in 1960 through the present moment in 1974. This is the age period in which a young man, according to ancient beliefs, must separate from the mother figure and enter into his adulthood leaving behind his childhood notions. Simon's rupture with the maternal universe surfaces by his writing and, finally, publishing this journal, in which he clearly delineates the harsh dichotomous reality that exists between two opposing political factions, men and women, in this cloistered milieu. He has freed himself from the bonds of academic policy, to keep the external world distant, and allowed the reader the opportunity to gaze into a secluded cosmos little known to outsiders. By permitting others to observe this closed society, Simon has broken from the profane domain of the maternal world, and this rupture hints that he has executed a venerated deed.

The name of Simon's wife, Lisa, could call to mind an allusion to the enigmatic portrait of Mona Lisa by Leonardo DaVinci in the sixteenth century. The mystery behind the identity of the woman has been explored since its first appearance. Giorgio Vasari, in his *Vite delle più eccellenti pittori, scultori ed architettori* (1550) identified the subject as, Lisa Gherardini, the third wife of Francesco del Giocondo, a silk merchant of Florence. However, it is the smile of this woman, both inviting and innocent that fascinates and mystifies the public. In a similar manner, Simon describes his wife as the Pisces woman who, like a fish, swims in two opposite directions, and, at the same time has an unfathomable smile,[36] that could parallel the mysterious facial expression of the Renaissance visual rendering.

Additionally, Simon describes her as "a daughter of the waves like Venus, thin-lipped and with a deep pubis" (73). These words are echoed in Rimanelli's mini memoir, *Molise Molise*.[37] In that text he describes his ex-wife, Bettina, as a "figlia dell'acqua come Venere," an idealized image of the female based on the famed Renaissance painting of Sandro Botticelli. This Botticelli image is one of three, and as such, a type of trilogy, much like the authors' English language books. The first of the paintings is known as the *Birth of*

---

[36] "Finally, I went out to my study across the meadow and brought back and acrylic painting which I myself made of her: a sweet face with an enigmatic smile, covered by enormous sunglasses" (27).

[37] Giose Rimanelli, *Molise Molise* (Isernia: Libreria Editrice Marinelli, 1979) 151.

Venus, the second, *Primavera* and the last, *Pallas and the Centaur*, all painted during the penultimate decade of the fifteenth century.

Yet, *Primavera*, the second of the trilogy, as is Rimanelli's *Accademia*, is, also, according to *La vita nuova*, the name that Dante gives to Giovanna, a friend of Beatrice, who, consequently, heralds only the coming and not the arrival, of his *donna angelicata*.[38] Rimanelli, therefore, possibly recognizes that his relationship with the second wife is not his apotheosis intimate link nor the glory and muse of his past literary works, but rather hints, as Dante does at the end of *La vita nuova*, that there is still much more to come in his artistic production.[39] At the same time, as Rimanelli makes the suggestion of a failed personal relationship in *Molise Molise*, Simon, in *Accademia*, also recognizes the same unfavorable fruition. Moreover, within this narrative of the author, there is a specific reference to Dante when Lisa remembers a poem Simon had written for her entitled *New Life*.

IX

Simon's poem should evoke in the reader Dante's book *La vita nuova*. The Florentine informs his reader, at the very start, that it is a *libro de la mia memoria* (19). Paget Toynbee explains that *La vita*

---

[38] According to Dante, she is called *Primavera* because: "Quella prima è nominata Primavera solo per questa venuta d'oggi; ché io mossi lo imponitore del nome a chiamarla così Primavera, cioè prima verrà lo die che Beatrice si mostrerà dopo la imaginazione del suo fedele. E se anche vogli considerare lo primo nome suo, tanto è quanto dire 'prima verrà,' però che lo suo nome Giovanna è da quello Giovanni lo quale precedette la verace luce, dicendo: *Ego vox clamantis in deserto: parate viam Domini*." See, Dante Alighieri, *Vita nuova*. *Rime*, Fredi Chiappelli, ed. (Milano: Mursia, 1965) 55.

[39] "Sì che, se piacere sarà di colui a cui tutte le cose vivono, che la mia vita duri per alquanti anni, io spero di dicer di lei quello che mai non fue detto d'alcuna" (76).

nuova is the first autobiographical work of modern literature.[40] It tells the story, in first person singular, of the pure love that Dante has for Beatrice. It is the memory of an ideal love for the poet's *donna angelicata*. In an ironic manner, the story of Simon and Lisa is a variation of the love story. Dante alone writes his autobiographical account. The reader does not get to perceive any of Beatrice's direct reactions. In contrast, *Accademia* presents two different journals, written by two distinct persons: the first, from Simon; the second, from Lisa. They both discuss the disintegration of their fourteen-year relationship. Dante did not have an actual connection with Beatrice. However, whereas Dante's *little book of memory* is dedicated to his adored lady who had just died, the narrative of Simon and Lisa is one that deals with the death of a relationship. Additionally, the name Lisa could be a variation, and a play on the name of the prophet Elisha, the successor to Elijah, and the guide to the people into the Promised Land. Simon's wife, however, is not taking him into the heavenly zone by crossing the river Jordan, instead, she is leading him down a path that will thrust him into a political and social civil war within the academic community by plunging him into the river Acheronte.

In order for Dante to escape *Inferno*, he must, by necessity, cross the Acheronte, the first river in hell. Virgil, his master and author,[41] is his guide on his journey. In a similar manner, Simon is confronted with his voyage, however, it is now the author Rimanelli who makes his appearance within the third part of the book. Twenty years after the relationship of Simon and Lisa have dissolved, the author recognizes that he must now cross the Acheronte in order to

---

[40] Paget Toynbee, *Dante Alighieri: His Life and Works*, Charles S. Singleton, ed. (New York: Harper & Row, 1965) 160.

[41] "Tu se' lo mio maestro e 'l mio autore, / tu se' solo colui da cu' io tolsi / lo bello stilo che m'ha fatto onore" (*Inferno* I: 85-87).

progress with his life and find his way into paradise. Rimanelli visits with his friend, a Canadian born psychoanalyst, Dr. Ralph Pépin. However, Pépin will, like Charon with Dante, inform this lost soul that his path is another and that he is not destined to reside in hell.

Moreover, the name of this psychoanalyst reminds the reader of the French medieval king, Pepin the Short, son of Charles Martel and father of Charlemagne. Although not a great king, Pepin the Short continued the work of his father with the expansion of the Frankish Church and the infrastructure (feudalism) that would turn out to be the backbone of medieval Europe. His assumption to the crown and the title of Patrician of Rome were precursors of his son's coroneted investiture, which is seen as the founding of the Holy Roman Empire.

Dr. Pépin and Simon/Rimanelli have been friends since 1952 when they both went to the Arctic in a small, tin plane with the purpose of helping the Moravian missionaries. However, the two got lost in the frozen tundra and it was seven days until they were found. Now, forty years later, Dr. Pépin, seeing that Simon/Rimanelli is again, disoriented within another static area of his personal and professional life, suggests a guide for this lost author out of his personal and professional inferno: Svevo,[42] who will, like Virgil, serve as the master and author for the journey that Simon/Rimanelli are to undertake.

Italo Svevo composed his novel *La coscienza di Zeno*, like *Accademia*, following a linguistic and narrative style of stream of consciousness. He paints a sardonic image of Trieste and, in particular of his hero, an indifferent man who cheats on his wife and lies to his psychiatrist by trying to explain himself revisiting his memories. In a similar and yet varied way, Simon/Rimanelli shows the pungent fig-

---

[42] "Do as Svevo did. Write a book on it. Then bring it to me. I'm a collector of manuscripts" (157).

ure of the academician, in the small world of letters, also trying to elucidate himself from a past that he still hasn't been able to leave behind. The difference, however, is that this character is not attempting to be apathetic or untruthful about his personal history, but rather learn from it, so as to be able to move forward.

Robert Pogue Harrison explains in his study "Approaching the *Vita nuova*" that Dante's work is a "retrospective self-editing digest that prepares the way for another itinerary altogether."[43] Although *Accademia* seems to be a story of marital betrayal, the binary pathway of its narrative will take the reader on another route that will show Simon's orphic voyage through the halls of academia and, as such, will suggest a Dantean like reality within the ivy-covered universe.

In a structural congruency of this novel with the work of the Florentine, Rimanelli's variation on the Orphic journey of his protagonist appears in a memory sequence that takes place in chapter 9. As Simon ponders the letter that he received from his friend Ugo, his remembrances of his entire life come to mind:

> Everything took another course. We slipped into the groove. And to register the fall signified to descend into the Avernus, among the Furies. But one adjusted even to this state of affairs. (74)

Avernus was an ancient name for a crater near Cumae, Italy. It was believed to be the ingress to Hades. In Virgil's *Aeneid*, the Cumaean Sibyl was the guide to the underworld, its entry being at the nearby crater of Avernus. Aeneas employed her services before his descent to the lower world to visit his dead father Anchises, but she warned him that it was not an easy undertaking the return from

---

[43] Robert Pogue Harrison, "Approaching the Vita Nuova" in *The Cambridge Companion to Dante*, Rachel Jacoff, ed. (Cambridge: Cambridge University Press, 1993) 42.

the abyss.[44] If Sibyl is the guide for Aeneas through the underworld, then the reference to Simon's ex-wife becomes even more relevant. Rimanelli, again, inverts the traditional epic poem by showing that Simon's Roman ex-wife, Sibyl, is not the guide through hell, but rather the one who directs Lisa and Simon on their respective journeys through the avernus of their personal lives. Lisa perceives the revenge of this Sibyl through the figure of Sandro, the outward appearance of Cain in *Accademia*. However, Virgil's *Aeneid*, is written in the pre-Christian era and Virgil, as Dante states, "Nacqui sub Iulio" (*Inferno* I: 70). Virgil' Sibyl, therefore, is not the one who escorts Simon on his trip through inferno, but rather, she is Dante's version of the Cumae, written in the Christian era.

The description of Simon's plunge into an inferno like reality within the academic community is strongly reminiscent of Dante's descent and is comparable within the nuances of the narrative. The evening in which he and his colleagues gather to watch the film the *Twelfth Macaque*, Simon describes the ambiance in the house as; "The smoke had had a hallucinatory effect on all our minds, but the effect seemed also to be boredom." (48) It is at this point in which Simon, searching for Lisa, goes down the stairway and finds her in a compromising position with two other people. However, the portrayal of Simon's ultimate fall into the dark underworld of sexual politics reminds the reader of Dante's statement:

> Non era camminata di palagio
> là 'v' eravam, ma natural burella
> ch'avea mal suolo e di dume disagio. (*Inferno* XXXIV: 97-99)

It is in this last circle of Hell in which Dante enters the innermost

---

[44] Trojan, Anchises' son, the descent of Avernus is easy. "All night long, all day, the door of Hades stand open. / But to retrace the path, to come up to the sweet air of heaven, / That is labour indeed" (*Aeneid* 6:10).

zone of Cocytus named for the arch-sinner Judas. Here, betrayal is the sin that carries man to the depths of *Inferno*. Simon's film tells the allegorical story of treachery. He perceives that Lisa will deceive him, specifically, with Guido Shait, an art professor who, in the film is called G.O and, although not recognizable to anyone in the audience, is made to appear as a Judas figure. Simon, moreover, does not see that he, too, has betrayed the bonds of marriage with Lisa. He has had several extramarital affairs but seems to be able to justify his actions, and not hers. Simon, the original name of Saint Peter who denies, three times, knowing Jesus after Judas denounced him, is in a comparable manner refusing to see that he too has rejected his life with Lisa and, at the same time, is unwilling to believe that he could be betrayed by her. However, it is Lisa's perfidy that will be more profound because it carries with it a binary purpose: the end of the intimate relationship with Simon; and, at the same time, she will manipulate the situation as to make Simon guilty in the eyes of the female constituency of his academic world. She, therefore, transports the personal problem into the professional sphere which will take him on his journey into the abyss of an academic inferno in which the faculty is divided along sexual/political lines: males and females.

The prominence of Dante in the works of Rimanelli is not uncommon, and it is perceptible within all his narratives within the specificity of the text.[45] Here, too, in *Accademia,* the reader is met by yet another savor of the Florentine and, once again, it is detected within the details of saga.

According to Dante and the medieval tradition, the number three is of great importance and consequence. Christopher Ryan, in his essay *The Theology of Dante*, states the gravity of the number:

---

[45] See my *Crossing the Acheron.*

> For Dante, the striving of the human being both to come to individual perfection in knowledge and love, and to reach the perfection in and through a community, has its source in the already perfect life of the Trinity.[46]

Structurally, *Accademia* is a novel in three parts with, three different narrators: Simon, Lisa, and the author Rimanelli. Simon informs the reader that he has experienced death on three separate occasions: the Italian Civil War; the end of his first marriage to Sibyl prompting his departure from Italy to come to America and start his academic career; and now, the end of his personal relationship with Lisa that he identifies will come shortly. Each of these death experiences occur, according to Simon's computations, every fifteen years. These horrific moments in his personal life started when he was twenty and have continued to the present, a span of thirty years; he is now entering the third cycle of his fifteen-year emotional death watch. Professionally, Simon is also having a difficult time with three women: Judy Madison, the soon to be ex-wife of his best friend and faculty member at the college who wants to have a sexual non-involved relationship with Simon; Charlotte Shark who wants to see Simon thrown out of the College; and, Lisa, who believes herself to be an academician, although not finished with her studies, at an equal par as her husband. Additionally, there are three females who are creating havoc in his personal life: Cress, his mother-in-law; Rose, the female student with whom Simon had an affair; and Lisa, his wife who believes that if Simon could betray her, she, also, has the right to do it. Simon's mother-in-law has been in three relationships: two with Italian men and the third, her husband, is a teacher of French; Rose becomes the third component in a marital triangle;

---

[46] Christopher Ryan, "The Theology of Dante," in *The Cambridge Companion to Dante*, 151.

and Lisa dreams of a ménage à trois with Rose as the third party.

In his novel *Graffiti*, the narrative traces the homicide of the protagonist's landlady, la signorina Laura Petracca. Italian Medieval and Renaissance culture and her rich literary tradition have played a unique role in the works of Rimanelli and, in that novel, the influence of the major writers is apparent. Rimanelli takes the classic Italian tradition of the *stilnovisti* and their view of *la donna angelicata* and inverts the figure to portray her counterpoint *la donna diabolica* in order to present a saturnine, biting look at contemporary society and the emerging and blossoming role women should play in it, by using as a fount the three major writers of Italy's literary past: Dante, Petrarca, and Boccaccio.

Lisa is not Simon's *donna angelicata* but rather, as in *Graffiti*, his *donna diabolica*. She has conducted him to the Acheronte with the purpose of leaving him in that deplorable place. Dante describes it as the land of the envious.[47] Lisa is a victim of her own pride. She is not at the same academic level as her husband and yet she recognizes that she is jealous of him. It is this resentment that creates the blind necessity, on her part, to destroy him.

> [...] I was becoming your enemy. Even if I had not gone to see her personally, Judy would have attended to this matter on her own and Susie, in turn, would have informed Charlotte, and Charlotte, Matthias. Soon the Cyrus Street world would be embracing a new sister and a divorce to boot. Revenge would be mine. (106-107)

She, erroneously, has blended the personal relationship that she has with Simon with that of his professional career. In her fits of envy, she turned to the female academicians within the College with the hope of destroying his life history. The animosity of the female col-

---

[47] "Questi non hanno speranza di morte, / e la lor cieca vita è tanto bassa, / che 'nvidïosi son d'ogne altra sorte" (*Inferno* III: 46-48).

leagues towards the male population on the campus will ignite the war between the sexes and Simon, an unwilling and uninvolved participant in this combat, will become one of its first victims.

Now, in the contemporary period, Simon/Rimanelli believes that he can finally free himself from the inferno in which Lisa attempted to keep him. He is guided across the Acheronte, finally, with the help of his Jewish American girlfriend. They are in Israel and she is entering a competition in which she will submit a proposal to reconstruct Noah's Ark. The Ark, the salvation of mankind, according to the Bible, will save Simon by carrying him across the waters of hatred and bigotry into a new consciousness in which self-interest and inflated egos will not exist in his new world.

According to Genesis, depravity and selfishness are more natural to man than decency and altruism. Ten generations after Adam and Eve the world became infused with decadence and revulsion. G-d is so grieved by their behavior that he regrets ever having given man life. He decides, therefore, to demolish all humankind, with the exception of Noah and his family, who he saw as a righteous man. However, Noah's reputation suffers because he does not inform anyone of G-d's plan. He builds the Ark cognizant that humanity will be destroyed. Simon, on the other hand, is informing the world of the horrors he endured within the confines of the academic universe with the purpose of creating a change within its contemporary political landscape. He points out that it is the misuse of predisposed power that created "the woods" (149) in which he was lost; his personal *selva oscura*, in which he found himself alienated and helpless for so many years.

Giose Rimanelli's novel *Accademia* appears to deal with the sexual conduct of a post-World War II generation in the world of university letters in which the politics of a lost war, Vietnam, invaded and infiltrated every part of a person's life. It, however, goes far beyond this simple chronicle of a failed marriage and the various sexual escapades of these characters. The author does not criticize the female populace; he uses them in an allegorical manner so that he may attack the ever present misuse of politics that have penetrated the world of academia and, ultimately, the inhumanity of a misguided few over the masses. His novel takes the reader into a domain rarely seen: the ivory towers and the daily political intrigue that encompasses it. In order to persuade the reader that nothing and no one is safe from this perversion, he juxtaposes the present time with the historical past to show the perennial Orphic voyage of his protagonist. Rimanelli, starting with *Tiro al piccione* and continuing through all his narratives, Italian and English, has attempted to highlight the political and social misuse of power that has had a firm grip on mankind. Unfortunately, according to *Accademia*, this political exploitation has even entered the world of academia, which should be void of any biased opinions, and the outcome is, always, the same: humanity suffers.

The Long and Winding Road in Giose Rimanelli's *The Three-Legged One*

Giose Rimanelli's recently released new English novel, *The Three-Legged One*,[1] is not an easy text for the novice. It is a challenging, intricate, and complex narrative that may well, simultaneously, confound and misdirect the experienced reader attempting to penetrate its simple, yet arcane facade. The novel, originally composed in the 1970s (but updated in the 1990s), now in the light of the twenty-first Century, projects an extremely negative and stereotypical, politically incorrect image of overly educated and sexually aggressive women, sex driven and domineering men, and spouse-swapping open marriages within the sheltered and protected ivory-covered sanctified walls of the American University system. Marital betrayal, in this contemporary fairy-tale like nightmare, is commonplace within the personal and professional arena and no one seems to be immune to its infection. Images of sexual violence, gratuitous sex, pedophilia, and personal and professional animosities bombard you in a saga that transcends the confines of marital discord and disintegration and enters into the realm of universal violence that inundated the second half of the 20th century, specifically, the twelve year period that commences with the assassination of the President of the United States and culminates with the resignation of another; the voyage from the idyllic Camelot of the Kennedy years to the depths

---

[1] Giose Rimanelli, *The Three Legged-One* (New York: Bordighera Press, 2008). All citations that come directly from this edition will be placed between parentheses within the body of the text.

of the political inferno of the Nixon/Watergate disaster that almost destroyed the nation.

This novel, the third English narrative of this Italian born writer, forms the final part of a trilogy that initiates with *Benedetta in Guysterland*, and is quickly followed by *Accademia*.² The trio of narrations will embrace two distinct decades in the span of the author's artistic life in his espoused new homeland, the United States, and, will encompass the major determinative and detrimental conflicts of their distinct eras: Vietnam, equal rights, and Watergate, each of which played a sizeable and critical role in the evolution of the social and cultural psyche of a nation.

Rimanelli, already an recognized part of the world of Italian letters of the post civil war years in the peninsula with his inaugural novel *Tiro al piccione*, moves to the United States at the very start of the 1960s, a decade that he describes in his Italian anecdotal text, *Tragica America*, as "il decennio piú tormentato della storia dopo l'unificazione e il New Deal.³" The 1970s, the period in which each of these novels occur are, by definition, an extension of the sociopolitical turbulent 60s. The chaotic and frantic years of the 1960s, the social unrest, the disillusionment with government policies that took the populace into an unending and unjustified war in Southeast Asia, the increased influence of the women's movement, and the advances in civil rights, all progress, although haltingly, into the 70s and have, by this period in time, gained a wider and even somewhat mainstreamed acceptance in this new decade, yet they are still rejected by the authoritarian classes.

---

² *Benedetta in Guysterland* (Montreal: Guernica Press, 1993); *Accademia* (Toronto: Guernica, 1997).
³ *Tiro al piccione* (Milan: Mondadori, 1953 [Turin: Einaudi, 1991]); *Tragica America* (Genova: Immordino editore, 1968) 7.

"Giose Rimanelli's *The Three-Legged One*"

The three novels, moreover, concentrate on different segments of this tumultuous decade: *Benedetta in Guysterland* deals with the initial years; *Accademia* and *The Three-Legged One* with the middle. In each case, it is the misuse and perversion of political power that propels this author to delve into its narrative reality by presenting a dark and somber vision of the universe in which he now lives: an American reality in which blind acceptance to overt magisterial power is no longer accepted without inquiry and debate and civil disobedience becomes the norm of the day.

In his first novel of this trilogy, *Benedetta in Guysterland*, the linguistic process penetrates the text while undergoing a maturation that expands within each passing chapter to present a narrative that develops into a new genre, the liquid novel. Rimanelli's *liquid novel* takes the traditional European narration, a formula that commenced *in illo tempore* with the storyteller, and transposes it into a new American paradigm by reformulating and reconstructing the configuration and language of the tale. He takes away the author from the narrative, for being excessive, and the text is, therefore, controlled by the reader who is being guided by the linguistic process from within. The fable has, therefore, been reinvented. Language has taken the place of the narrator.

At the same time, *Benedetta in Guysterland*, like Rimanelli's first Italian narrative, *Tiro al piccione*, is an antiwar document that plays with the concept of time by repositing temporal frames between two distinct eras: the Fascist period in Italy that brought the nation into a horrific civil war and in the United States, the generational fraction that existed during the Vietnam era that brought forth a *quasi* civil war ambiance.[4]

---

[4] Sheryl Lynn Postman "A Cracked Mirror, A Fragmented History and A Path that Always Comes Back to the Beginning: Giose Rimanelli's *Benedetta in Guysterland*," *Forum Italicum* 41.1 (Spring 2007): 79-110.

Accademia, like its predecessor, throws the reader immediately, into a hastily moving and continuously altering vortex of a new relevant and confrontational era in American history that shaped another civil war-like atmosphere in the nation: the Equal Rights Movement. According to the author's text, socio-politics, which should not be a part of the Academic community, have filtered into its cloistered community and hindered the growth of the male scholar, forcing that person to live within a gender controlled and subjugated hell from which his escape is unlikely. Coincidently, three years after the events of *Accademia* take place, in 1977, the author published his book *Graffiti*, which like the aforementioned novel, presents a tale in which sexual politics plays a dominant role. Rimanelli, in that experimental Italian tale, creates a unparalleled and acerbic satire on the ever varying persona of women and the enduring infernal in which men are restrained to live if they resist to accept this new view. In brief, as men move into the twenty-first century, they are objurgated to damnation if they do not leave behind, rightly so in the past, their primitive concepts of women.[5]

Rimanelli, as he did with his earlier narrative, *Accademia*, exhibits in *The Three-Legged One,* the American University community engulfed in an environment of darkness and despair. The cultural existence with all its oddities and intricacies play out in this narrative and preside over the current time. To highlight the fear and deprivation of confidence that exists in the present era in his new collective academic atmosphere, Rimanelli threads within the current text corresponding situations of panic and fright that propelled Europe and, specifically, the Italian peninsula, thirty years earlier, into its bloody infernal of the Civil War. The writer, conscious of his Italian medieval literary education, counter positions the present-day historical

---

[5] For more on this topic, please see my study in: *Crossing the Acheron: A Study of Nine Novels by Giose Rimanelli* (New York: Legas Publishing, 2000) 147-67.

period with the appalling world of the Fascist era that absorbed the peninsula from 1922-1945.

Simultaneously, the author punctuates this tale of political distrust with a horrific moment of American history: the 1891 lynching of Italians in New Orleans and the criminally responsible role that the government played in allowing for this tragedy to take place. The impetus, therefore, for this novel, *The Three-Legged One,* was a defining moment in American domestic governmental politics that still echoes today in the 21st century: Watergate, and the wariness of the populace toward the administration and its elected officials for having lied and covered up their deceit to the American people. He then, carefully, juggles two dissimilar historical eras within two unlike universes at two extremely critical moments in their social and political developments.

In order for the author to engender the required bigeminal passageway to usher us along through the social and political perdition of the 1970s, he must set in relief two specific time stages of analogous dismay: the European power struggle of the pre and World War II years; and the 70s, a period in which the young people of the American university were now questioning their authoritative political figures in a world metamorphosing, and their sexual freedom that became a weapon in a personal arsenal that blinded the individual to issues of trust and confidence, which in turn reverberated in the view the young had of their legislative representatives. Additionally, to highlight the binary passage of civil upheaval of this era, the author establishes, from the novel's inception, the duality of the text by setting in relief two contrary elements: male/female; Italy/United States; personal/ professional life; and the sheltered life of the University/ the exposed worldwide community.

The temporal dislodging occurs one day in which Simon reads a letter from, Ugo, his friend from Italy. His companion informs him about the political fiascos taking place in Italy, and equates it to a Neapolitan farce comedy that engrosses and entertains the public. At the same time, Ugo is concerned that the aftermath of this disaster will plunge the country into a deeper cultural dilemma, allowing for terrorism to take a foothold in the peninsula. At the conclusion of his letter, Ugo asks him about his life in America. While pondering the correspondence Simon refers to Vera being absent, in New York with her mother, and that with her out of town, he is left remembering his entire life.[6]

Coincidentally, this time alone will allow for Simon to embark upon a transcendental voyage through several time periods of his life which will bombard him with images from his past. As he continues reading the correspondence from Ugo, he becomes aware that sleep is a distraction from the solitude he endures with Vera away:

> Remembrance is the only presence, along with sleep. I sleep more than ever when she's not here, weariness accumulates and sleep shakes it off. I gently indulge in ironic self-reflection, observing my face in profile. (79)

The journey that the protagonist makes, is in a type of hypnogogic state, and is one that agrees with Eliade's concept of *dream time*: a return to the start, *ab initio*, of creation; man must re-create the myth, *illo tempore*, of his own beginnings (*imago mundi*). Dream

---

[6] This house is vast and narrow, it seems to be made of furniture, of objects. But when she's here it seems to be an extension of her self, and even time is no longer with me, she makes me act. But time is a vague cognition; the writer finds it by isolating himself, the lover by exhibiting himself, by talking, by caressing. The best time is always that spent with another person, the worst is with a blank sheet of paper staring at you and the memory that fills it. It is a time-frame as narrow and vast as this house (78).

time endows man to integrate again the sacred time of the commencement of things, and, therefore, to renew the world.[7]

The memory comes to light as Vera takes the bus from Anaconda to New York City. This enormous reptile that extends for several feet is known for its sleek and stealthy manner in which it maneuvers and navigates through the swamps of the Amazon, and it is the journey of this boa, the snake, that, ultimately, transports Simon *ab initio*, to the beginning of time:

> One of these days you'll abandon daddy and you will become Eve. Eve is already preformed in the Garden, and the serpent already exists in the Garden. (31)

Mircea Eliade states that a myth connects a sacred history, a primal occurrence that took place *ab initio*. The allegory is history that took place, *in illo tempore*. Once told, the enigma becomes an unconditional legitimate action; it constitutes a validity that is unequivocal.[8] If, however, as Eliade states, myth is always the recital of a creation and it speaks only of realities, then the myth that Rimanelli is trying to uncover is man's ability to deceive another, and the Watergate scandal in which the President of the United States pretended not to be involved, is the paradigm of an inflated ego in a person whose criminal actions nearly destroyed the tranquility of the nation.

The reference to this outrage is perceived within the specificity of the text. Vera tells Simon of a sexual episode that she witnessed one day in the library. A young man touches himself while looking at a girl. Vera believes that the female is Roseanne, the women with whom Simon had an affair and the reason for which Vera is now

---

[7] Mircea Eliade, *Rites and Symbols of Initiation*, translated from the French by Willard R. Trask (New York: Harper Torchbooks, 1958) 6.

[8] Mircea Eliade, *The Sacred and The Profane*, translated from the French by Willard R. Trask (New York: Harcourt Brace Jovanovich, 1959) 95.

emotionally blackmailing him. Simon decides to verify the information:

> "I've got to phone her," you said, suddenly.
> "Why, don't you believe me?"
> "I'd like to confirm it."
> It was, however, already late, we followed the discussions on Watergate on TV... (140)

Historically, the period in which this novel takes place is the time of the Watergate scandal. This era saw a governmental administration committing illegal activities, abuses and crimes against the nation. The scandal reached to the top levels of the Administration and it was the attempted cover-up of the action that ultimately caused the resignation of the President. Richard Nixon believed himself to be above the law and, therefore, innocent of any sin. The notion that man is equal to G-d and not bound by any rules is the basis for which man was exiled from Eden; it also proved to be the reason for which Nixon was brought up on impeachment charges and for which he, ultimately, resigned. The lack of trust permeates, at this point in time, through all phases of the American psyche, both governmental and personal.

The institute of higher education in both *Benedetta in Guysterland* and *Accademia* is Anabais College. The name evokes in the reader the classic work of Greek literature by Xenophon. Although that tale recounts the story of a large Greek army hired by Cyrus the Younger to seize, from his brother Artaxerex II, the throne of Persia, the term itself has come to refer to a long journey. However, in this newest edition of the trilogy, the name of the institute has changed. It is now Anaconda.

An anaconda is a reptile, a huge snake that belongs to the boa family. It lives in South America, predominantly in the tropical rainforests of the Amazon region. Although these snakes are known for their monumental size, they are not venomous. They coil their bodies around the captured prey and squeeze until the animal asphyxiates. They can swallow their target whole and go for weeks or months without food after a big meal. It is the manner by which this animal is able to move, sliding in and out of the marshes, that allows the transference between time periods: the past and the present.

In this newest part of the trilogy, the author makes an appearance as a character in the final section of the novel. In a conversation he has with the son of Simon, the main male character of the narrative, twenty years after the final episode of these diaries, there is a direct and specific reference to Rimanelli's first English novel, *Benedetta in Guysterland*:

> And the book? What did you call it, A Glossed Novel? C'mon, coward, tell him. It's called *The Three-legged One. A Glossed Novel* by... A book designed for sarcasm, parody of mores and moral in exchange for a few Bergsonian laughters, almost just like (not quite) the other one you wrote in English, *Benedetta in Guysterland. A Liquid Novel* by..." (189)

If, as the author states, this novel, *The Three-Legged One* is like *Benedetta in Guysterland,* and uses a language as a means by which the author may detach himself from the narrative content and create a storyline in which, ultimately, language plays an essential function, then the disturbing and violent linguistic game plan strategy present in this tale is a means by which the author conveys the highly volatile and explosive emotional characteristics of an historic time period, Watergate, in which the American people were constantly on the verge of national hostilities.

This is, moreover, not the first time that there is an interplay between the author and a character within his literary opus. In his novel *Grafitti*,[9] the protagonist of that novel, Piero Lapulce has a dialogue with Marco Laudato, the author's alter ego and the protagonist of his first novel, *Tiro al piccione*. The presence of Marco Laudato in *Grafitti* is not gratuitous nor is it accidental. Twenty two years earlier, 1943-1945, Marco found himself in a parallel situation that confronts Piero: the civil unrest of a nation that ultimately plunged it into the hell of a war time condition, the Italian Civil War. Additionally, this character, Laudato, reappears in his short story collection, *Il tempo nascosto tra le righe*, in two accounts: *Fantasmi del passato* and *Dimostranti*.[10] Once again in these narratives, Marco Laudato is confronted with civil unrest; however, now a resident of the United States, Marco experiences the political, social, economic, racial and sexual unrest and revolutions of the 1960s.

The presence of the author now in this novel, *The Three-Legged One*, occurs twenty years after the final entries of the diaries. Again, the emergence of the writer is not haphazard. During his conversation with Daniel, Rimanelli finds out that the young man is HIV positive, the virus that causes AIDS. The era is 1994 and the public in general does not know how to deal with this malady. Most people, incorrectly, assume that this is a "homosexual disease" and not attributable to the heterosexual community. Companies and corporations are dismissing employees for fear that the illness is transmitted in an airborne manner.[11] Fear outweighs logic; prejudice, towards the gay community, is rampant. Fifty years earlier,

---

[9] Giose Rimanelli, *Graffiti*, a cura di Titina Sardelli (Isernia: Editrice Marinelli, 1977).

[10] Giose Rimanelli, *Il tempo nascosto tra le righe* (Isernia: Editrice Marinelli, 1986) 137-68.

[11] In 1993 the film *Philadelphia*, directed by Jonathan Demme and written by Ron Nyswaner, premiered. The basic story is that a successful man with AIDS, an attorney on the path to partnership, is fired by his conservative law firm because of his condition. The man sues the firm, wins the case, and unfortunately, at the end, dies.

"Giose Rimanelli's *The Three-Legged One*"

Giose/Marco Laudato was forced to fight, on the wrong side, in a Civil War in which his native Italy was nearly destroyed. Daniel, the son of Simon, a victim of the HIV virus is, also, on the opposite side of an issue: life or death, and he, too, must fight. Daniel's battle, like Marco's fifty years earlier, is for his very existence. His contact with the disease, which as he states is a constant struggle, is suggested to have been caused by a life style, opposite to the one that Simon has endured. The reference to Daniel's malady, moreover, returns the reader to Simon's journal entry, and away from the author's attendance, to the temporal shifting that occurred with the missive that he received from Ugo, "the gentlest homosexual I have ever encountered in the world" (xvii).

The elemental story of *The Three-Legged One* is simple, although the tale behind the veil is much more complicated. A professor of physical anthropology at Anaconda University, in upstate New York, and his wife are suffering a severe marital meltdown. The couple has been together for fourteen years. Simon Dona is an Italian born scholar, writer and documentary filmmaker from the region of Selimo. Vera, his wife, is a native born American from New Canaan, Connecticut, a Ph.D. candidate writing her dissertation on Spencer. She is the result of an illicit affair that her mother had with an Italian sailor prior to WWII. Through the course of Vera and Simon's union, they have been intermittently plagued by her mother and Vera's perpetual requisite to control the bond with Simon by means of sentimental extortion. To break loose of the mother's firm grip on her daughter, Simon takes a position at the University of British Colombia in Vancouver, Canada, on the opposite side of the North American continent. After a few years Vera demands to return to the United States. Simon then accepts a faculty position in California at UCLA. Vera, pregnant, before the journey to Vancouver, gives birth to a son, Daniel, in Connecticut.

She leaves the new born child with her mother, threatening Simon with divorce if he insists on keeping the child and taking it away from her mother. Several years go by and, once again, Vera wants to move, this time, geographically closer to her mother. Simon finds new employment at Anaconda University, not far from Vera's mother's home (three hours), where their baby is being raised. He refuses to visit the son because of his mother-in-law. Over the course of the next few years, the twosome becomes friends with several members of the academic community. They have each had sexual experiences outside the confines of their marriage. However, although they do not believe that they have an open marriage, they believe that absolute truth is necessary for their relationship to continue. Eventually, Vera finds out that Simon is having an affair with a younger female student and, then, in an effort to continue her control of the matrimonial connection, begins to emotionally pressure her husband: first insisting, to Simon's mortification, on a *ménage à trois* with the very female student with whom Simon had the affair; and then proposing that she, too, would commence a sexual relationship with a man other than her spouse. Each suggestion causes more and more discord in their personal liaison. Ultimately, the couple divorce. Simon has disappeared from sight and no one knows if he is alive or dead.

Structurally the novel is divided into three parts, although the last segment, written twenty years after the first two parts, is brief and, ultimately, serves as a follow-up, albeit in a shroud, of the initial portion, and suggests that the author is, in fact, the missing Simon, now residing in Selinsgrove, Pennsylvania. The first two divisions are the "love diaries" of the main characters, Vera and Simon. They are narrated, predominantly, in the first person singular and allow the reader to actively, and, at the same time, passively participate in the disintegration of their marriage. Each section of the book is recounted by a different voice, however, the first two parts are edited by a third voice, R. Carmen Cara.

The main corpus of this new novel is the daily journals of the two spouses: Simon and Vera, and the unending psychological study of Cara regarding the entries by the spouses. The third part of the tale, the *Author's note*, introduces the novelist, Giose Rimanelli, as a Pirandello-like character into the text. Each storyteller, moreover, has a specific number of chapters and the first two segments are congruent to the other: ten chapters per voice; twenty subdivisions in all. At the same time, the two principle voices, Simon and Vera, subdivide into three voices each. Simon speaks in the first two chapters in the third person singular informing the reader, in fact, that he is the "I" of this narrative.[12] Later, in the fourth chapter, Simon employs the second person singular voice as he directs his comments to himself directly. The remaining part of his journal is written in the first person singular. Vera, at the same time, also utilizes three distinct voices. The largest section of her diary consists of her memories in the first person singular. Then there is the second person singular when she addresses comments directly to Simon. The third person singular is used when she makes statements regarding Simon.

The *Author's Note*, on the other hand, consists of one chapter and Rimanelli's appearance functions as a type of Dioneo, given license to speak about whatever he prefers and not being restrained to the events of the day. His narrative voice deals with the present moment in time, the 1990s, twenty years after the diaries, and although the story of Simon and Vera does not explicitly appear in this section, it is suggested by the appearance of Daniel. There are,

---

[12] "Academically, he is a physical anthropologist, the I of this Diary, better known in American university circles for the endless interpolations that his writings, based on endless interpolations that his writings, based on experiments with monkeys of the Macaque species in the Philippines and in Borneo (the rhesus monkeys, such as the mandril and the baboon) offer to the old adage:... " (7).

however, linguistic and stylistic game patterns that parallel Simon's and may lead one to believe that Simon and Rimanelli could be the same person.

Simon's chapters do not, apparently, follow a chronological design of discourse, as does Vera's. His narration is a stream of consciousness that creates a puzzle-like pattern in which time is fragmented and not lineal. The reference to dates appears hidden within the narrative of his journal and through these entries the reader becomes aware of the fact that they pre-date the start of a new academic year (1974) by three days. The only specificity to time appears in his first entry: August 21, 1974. However, Vera's entries are, for the most part, assigned a date and even a time of day. Although her story shifts between the present and the past, she is much more direct and specific than Simon. In addition, Vera's journal anticipates that of Simon's by sixteen months. Each segment of the journals, like chess pieces, has a specific destination and, therefore, can stand independently from the other chapter or collectively to assist in the physical and emotional shaping of the entire story. At the same time, R. Carmen Cara's commentaries create a third narrative within this narration and serve as a type of decorative border to the entire work, evoking for the reader the frame narrative elicited by Boccaccio.

The appearance of this third voice, Rex Carmen Cara, could, also, suggest to the reader the biblical passages of Solomon's *Song of Songs*. The full name of this arbitrator hints at the intertextual reference and reverence within the narrative: *Rex* meaning king; and *Carmen Cara*, a precious song. At the start of the book, Cara informs the reader that "These are love diaries" (7). The *Song of Songs*, traditionally, is handled as an allegorical representation of the relationship of G-d and Israel, and this kinship is depicted as husband and wife. Literally, however, the main characters of the verses are merely a man and a woman, and the poem suggests movement from courtship to consummation. The diaries that Cara presents are, temporally, specified as between 1960 and 1976: from the courtship of Vera and Simon until shortly after their divorce. Their sexual exploitations within their personal liaison and with others (real or in fantasy), play out on this canvas in graphic detail through the course of this narrative.

The link to King Solomon becomes even more perceptible within the commentaries of Cara. At the start of Vera's journal, this editor explains that although Vera's entries pre-date those of Simon, he felt personally bound to deal with his friends' diary first.[13] His refusal to take a side in the battle between the couple evokes the biblical episode of Solomon and the two prostitutes, each claiming that they were the true parent of a child. According to the episode Solomon suggests dividing the child in two with a sword. The true mother is revealed because she is willing to relinquish her child to the lying woman rather than have her child killed. Solomon, the judge, declares that the woman who showed compassion is the true mother and hands the child to her.[14] Cara, although the attorney who handled Simon's divorce from Vera, is attempting to, objectively, allow the reader to intuit an educational lesson from their discourse and, like Solomon, not play an active role in the decision.

---

[13] "The main reason for the time delay before devoting myself to Vera's labour is, perhaps, due to the fact that I pursued Simon's remembrances much more than I did Vera's. Physically she attracted me very much but I was honor-bound to respect Simon's friendship and the traditions that he cultivated. So I always repressed my sensuality in her presence even though we both played perilously with our respective sensualities. Truth to tell I was attracted more to him than to her so that she soon realized that there were other copulations, all of them stupendous but seasonal" (90).
[14] *1 Kings 3*: 16-28.

Rimanelli has stated that all his work is autobiographical in nature.[15] He does not engage, as George Gusdorf explains, as his own historian in this text.[16] There is no congruency between the narrator's voice, the writer's voice, and the protagonist. Nor is there, as Philippe Lejeune states, an autobiographical pact.[17] There are, however, elements within this narrative that correspond to the author's life. Both Simon and Rimanelli fought on the wrong side of a political civil war; both have a Canadian mother, a devout Catholic who wanted her son to become a member of the Church; both, also, are one of three children; each has a maternal grandfather who came from New Orleans; and both were captured and imprisoned in Villafranca (Mantua). However, there are significant disparities between the two. Simon comes from the region of Selimo, Italy and Rimanelli, from the region of Molise. Selimo is an obvious anagram of the

---

[15] "My literature is almost all autobiographical in nature: novels, poetry, literary criticism. I date everything I write; on each completed work I mark down the hour, the day, the month and the year. And this is because I feel I am alone in the world. My writing, in fact, has never been directed at the world, rather, it reflects the reality of my own existence in direct contact with practical facts or ideals offered by my world's historical contingencies. My discourse, therefore, is more narrative than critical, more personal than objective. I learn by writing. " (Giose Rimanelli, "Notes on Fascist/Antifascist Politics and Cultures from the Point of View of a Misfist," *Rivista di Studi Italiani* 2 (Dec. 1984): 73.
Rimanelli echoes these same ideas within this present text. However, now instead of the author citing this passage, it is Daniel, the son of Simon, who reminds the author of his speech at the University of Bologna (April 9, 1984). Daniel, criticizing the author, reminds him that Giose always claims to be writing the truth: "How do you call it, Truth? Well, yes, and I hope you didn't forget what you said in a speech at the University of Bologna, April 9, 1984, claiming that your "literature is almost all autobiographical in nature: novels, poetry, literary criticism," etcetera, with that making clear, crystal clear that any for of autobiography tells the truth. Is this the truth, the whole truth? Hell, No!" (189)
[16] George Gusdorf, "Conditions and Limits of Autobiography," in *Autobiography*, edited by James Olney (Princeton University Press: Princeton, 1980) 31.
[17] Philippe Lejeune, *On Autobiography* (University of Minnesota Press: Minneapolis, 1989) 5.

author's home province and this juxtaposition of the letters of the area are meant to disassociate himself, physically and spiritually, with the region of his youth. Additionally, Simon's father, a descendent of a heraldic family, was Jewish, a Rabbi, forced to convert to Christianity in order to preserve the family line. Rimanelli's father was Catholic and the first child of an illegitimate peasant whose name was created, at his birth, as an anagram to the surname of the biological father, Marinelli.[18]

At the same time, both Simon and Rimanelli were married twice with each having three sons, two from the first wife and one from the second. However, neither of the sons' names corresponds to the author's children nor does the name of the second wife agree. The differences, although apparently minor, are sufficient to deny any type of autodiegetic pact between the character created in this tale and the writer and they, ultimately, reverberate the ideas of Antonio Porta and Tzvetan Todorov at the start of the narrative.[19] Giovanni Cecchetti, also, points out that Rimanelli composes narratives that deal with himself only in appearance. He adds that the writer mythifies not only himself but everyone around him.[20] The author, therefore, gleans information from his own personal life and then extends it to his artistic creation. Additionally, in the third section of the book, the *Author's note*, the character, Giose, informs us that Cara has held hostage his manuscript, for twenty years, and only now, with the death of the lawyer, three months earlier, has he been

---

[18] Conversations with the author. See, also, Giose Rimanelli, *Familia* (Isernia: Iannone, 2000).

[19] Antonio Porta, in his poem *Cara*, states: "In order to decide I chose a different name..."; and Tzvetan Todorov, in his work *Literature and Signification*, states: [...] where the story that is narrated ends, is precisely where the story that narrates, the literary story begins" (*The Three-Legged One*, 1).

[20] Giovanni Cecchetti, "Autobiografia mitografica in Giose Rimanelli," in *Rimanelliana*, edited by Sebastiano Martelli (Stony Brook: FLibrary, 2000) 123.

able to get hold of it. The implication is apparent: the absent Simon of the 1970s, is the alter ego of the present day Giose Rimanelli.

The appearance in the *Author's Note* of the adult Daniel also assists in the novel's binary passageway of linking the past with the present. Biblically, Daniel, the interpreter of dreams, was the advisor to Nebuchadnezzar, the ruler of Babylon from 605 B.C. to 562 B. C. The *Book of Daniel*, written in Aramaic and Hebrew, is a text with two distinct parts: the first section deals with court stories which focus on religious fidelities involving Daniel and his friends and the interpretation of royal dreams; the second part of the book deals with his reception of dreams, visions and angelic interpretations that are written in the first person singular voice.

Daniel's presence, twenty years in the future, serves to remind the reader of the distinction that exists between fiction and autobiography. The narrative consists of two distinct parts: the continuation, in the guise of Daniel, of the saga initiated with the writings of Simon and Vera; and the reality of the author and his interplay with his fictional character. At the same time, it transports the author to another time in which, indirectly, he is now free to interpret the past in its proper context. Memory, which was hallucinatory for Simon, proves to be beneficial and liberating for Rimanelli; the nightmare is finally over.

Concurrently, the incubus that Rimanelli surpasses and that Simon endures reminds the reader of the terrifying and nightmarish years of the Watergate ignominy and the unending inferno in which the American populace plunged because of the nefarious deeds of the Nixon Administration. Upon assuming the presidency of the United States on August 9, 1974, the day after Nixon's resignation, Gerald Ford told the nation in his inaugural speech, "My fellow Americans, our long national nightmare is over." However, the perpetual shadow of the Watergate outrage and dishonor does not come to a final respite until April, 1994 with the death of Richard M. Nixon, twenty years after his resignation.

This time frame, moreover, equates to the occurrence of Daniel and the writer in this contemporary novel. Rimanelli's saga initiates in 1973 with the journal entries of Vera at the height of the Watergate investigations. Simon's tale commences on August 21, 1974, thirteen days after the resignation of the President. The entire book comes to a close in the Spring of 1994, twenty years after the demise of a marriage between two academicians and, likewise, twenty years after the death of a union between a nation and the President of the United States.

Gerald Ford's declaration of the conclusion of the country's nightmare suggested a possible bridge between the nation's devastating recent past and the encouraging near future. Daniel's attendance is, simultaneously, a span between the two diverse worlds of the author at two distinct times. Daniel is present in Simon and Vera's journals of the 1970s and he is a tangible link with the author in the present time. The dichotomous nature of the narration, therefore, holds true.

Throughout Rimanelli's writings, his parent's home has generally been the center of his universe. However, by 1994, the year in which this novel was finally completed, both parents have passed away,[21] and there no longer survived, as in past times, a personal bond with Molise, Canada or Detroit. The deficiency of this personal solidified association would demand, by definition, the inversion of Molise into Selimo; the liaison, albeit physically broken, is still expressively and psychologically attached. Rimanelli published, in 1979, his mini memoir *Molise Molise,*[22] as a tribute to his home re-

---

[21] Vincenzo Rimanelli died on August 8, 1988 and Concettina Rimanelli died on October 13, 1993.
[22] Giose Rimanelli, *Molise Molise* (Isernia: Marinelli, 1979).

gion. In a strange twist of reality, Carmen Cara informs the reader that Simon published his autobiography, *Selimo Selimo* one year earlier than Rimanelli's tale. This inversion of the regions' name from Molise into Selimo mirrors the author's personal history and the creation of his own surname: Marinelli anagrammed into Rimanelli.

The reader of Rimanelli's work will also recognize the identification of Selimo as not being uncommon and it brings to mind his poem, *La ballata di Joe Sèlimo*, from his book *Moliseide*.[23] In his introduction to Rimanelli's collection of poems, Luigi Bonaffini makes clear that the author sees himself with the character Joe Sèlimo and that the epic is a state of consciousness that connotes compenetration of factual visual images in the illusory fabric of imagination (xix). The author insinuates the sanctity that a small, enclosed space offers to his persona by comparing it to the world at large. Within its restricted, geographic limits, Joe is able to travel across time and space, thereby attesting to their intermingling and the harmonious blending between these two distinct concepts. This idea runs in a parallel manner in Rimanelli's current literary work and is brought to light by the author's reference, at the very start of the narration, to the study, a separate room within the fraudulent sacred world of his house, in which he writes his journal. Through the course of Simon's diary the reader is taken on a journey through time, a voyage that transcends the chronological and enters into the mythic, having the male character depart from this profane area and, ultimately, depositing him, possibly, in an uncontaminated beatified zone where he can start anew.

The emergence of Simon Dona in *The Three-Legged One* is not the first time that the reader of Rimanelli's opus is confronted

---

[23] "Sono chiuso in una stanza / piccolina come il mondo. / Rido e danzo, a volte piango, / sono intenso come il mondo. / Alla fine, rassegnato / ho sposato l'emozione."

with this persona. His appearance, first in *Accademia*, and then in another novel, *Detroit Blues*, takes place in the same year, 1997. This latter book, written in Italian, dealt with the race riots that took place in the Motor City in 1967. In that work of fiction Simon Dona's name was more Italian, Simone Donato, and it appears that over the course of the seven years from which *Detroit Blues*[24] occurs until this novel (1974), the protagonist's name has become more Americanized.

In the Italian novel, Simone is, like Simon, a professor of Anthropology. However, the difference is that Simone taught at the University of California Berkeley, whereas Simon taught at the University of California Los Angeles. Simon does not move to New York until after the riots and so the mention of Anaconda University would not appear in the earlier narration which pre-dates the change of residence. Simone is from the small Apennines region of Molise, Italy, and Simon claims to be from the small region of Selimo, Italy. At the same time, the female figure in *Detroit Blues*, physically absent throughout the text, is Simone's wife, Lisa. Simon's wife in *Accademia* is, also, named Lisa (Jones). However, in this newest apparition of the character, the name of the wife is now Vera Jones.

Another divergent element appears in this third incarnation of the Dona family history: a commentator, R. Carmen Cara, and his presence explains the subtitle of the book, *A Glossed Novel*, and it is through his detailed notes and commentaries that the reader has a greater understanding of the characters and times in which they live. In his observations that accompany this newest text, the reader is informed that Simon's wife, Vera, is actually named Guendalisa Jones (p. 234) and this would, therefore, suggest that the Lisa of *Accademia* and *Detroit Blues* is, in fact, the same person. Further-

---

[24] *Detroit Blues* (Welland, Ontario: Editions Soleil, 1997).

more, Cara informs the reader that Lisa's middle name is Vera, thereby tying together the characters of the earlier novels with the present narrative.

In *Accademia*, Simon is a professor at Anabasis College in Nabokov County, Appalachia. In his novel *Benedetta in Guysterland*, this same small town is described as being primeval in demeanor and in language. Much like the other protagonists' home area in the author's previous books, Appalachia is located in the mountainous regions of mid-America, while Molise, coincidentally, is in the central part of the Italian peninsula in the Matese mountain range. The depiction of daily life in this small rural community of the United States is interchangeable to the one that the author attributes to his home area in Italy and both are geographically separated, and distant, from all major cities thereby forming a world unto itself.

Now in *The Three-Legged One*, Simon is a professor at Anaconda University in upstate New York. His social position, professionally and personally, is the same as in *Accademia*, however, now the geographic locale has differed. Moreover, there is no physical or psychological rendering of this new locale.

Rimanelli's novels of the 1950s through the 1980s have either Molise, Canada or Detroit, the geographic regions where his parents reside, always serving as his sacred space. According to Mircea Eliade, the sacred is indistinguishable to a pious energy and to a divine truth (Eliade, 1959, 12). As his parents moved from Molise to Canada, and then Canada to Detroit, the beatified space for the author has also relocated. At the same time, within this sanctified, environmental zone, the parental house has always been reserved as his *axis mundi*.[25] It was in their house that either the news of the day, comings and goings of great importance, and safety from the outside

---

[25] Mircea Eliade, *Images and Symbols: Studies in Religious Symbolism* (New York: Sheed and Ward, 1969) 39.

elements (war and riots) protected the author. Profane space would, therefore, represent anything that subsisted outside the chosen, hallowed domain.

In Rimanelli's narratives, each time a character (Marco Laudato in *Tiro al piccione*, Nicola Vietri in *Peccato originale*,[26] Massimo Niro in *Una posizione sociale*,[27] Piero Lapulce in *Grafitti*, or Simone Donato in *Detroit Blues*) left the confines of the parents' home, the reverent space, the protagonist was confronted with the venomous and cruel realism of civil war, hatred, bigotry and violence.

Simon, in describing Anaconda University, seeks to establish parallel reverent terms in order to suggest the sanctity of this center of higher education,[28] however, all his endeavors fall greatly short in this his final position within an academic environment. Anaconda, as its namesake suggests, has a tight strangle hold on the faculty. Like the reptile, whose eyes are on top of the head allowing them to lay in wait for their prey while remaining nearly completely submerged and unseen, the entire faculty of Anaconda University observes every little detail of each member in its community. Then, once a target is chosen, they pounce on their victim causing professional pain and destruction. Jealousy among these professionals is rampant and so too are their insecurities. They are state employees who need to solicit funds from outside sources in order to do their research. The state is unable to support them in an adequate manner. To acquire financial support, Simon has been known to produce short films.

---

[26] Giose Rimanelli, *Peccato originale* (Milan: Mondadori, 1954).
[27] *Una posizione sociale* (Florence: Vallechi. 1959).
[28] [...] The Academy was the mother, and to her they attributed guilt and wonder, loss and self modesty, death and metaphor, justice and purity, intentionality and cowardice, hope and judgment, ideology and humorism, obligation and desperation, faith and malice, rite and ecstasy, obsession and discourse. And sentimentalism to boot (11).

Anna Madison is an entomologist who studies the life of cockroaches and is the ex-wife of Simon's friend and collaborator, Andrew. In the course of her research, she has named each of the bugs in her laboratory after specific faculty members at the University. At the same time, Simon explains to Anna that in Rome, Italy, this is the same term, *bacarozzi*, that they use for priests. He has converted the sacred image of the religious person into the secular figure of a creepy crawly pest that has a perennial negative characteristic.

This unsanctified area of the church is a topic that echoes in some of the author's earlier works. The short story, *Due vocazioni* is the tale of a young protagonist, Lorenzo, who left his native homeland, Molise, to attend a religious school in order to become a man of the cloth. However, Lorenzo, ultimately, abandons his religious training and returns to his parents' home. Luigi Reina sees a blending between the autobiographical personalities shown in the character of Lorenzo Jasenza with that of *Tiro al piccione's* Marco Laudato.[29] Lorenzo's experiences in the seminary, which should, by definition, be sacrosanct, are shown to be blasphemous: students who dream of carnal experiences; priests who dictate and intimidate; inhuman treatment within the student body; inappropriate behavior unbecoming a (possible) religious person.[30]

It is Matthias Freedman, the University Vice President, however, who clearly points out the secular atmosphere that now has infiltrated the confines of this pseudo sacred place:

> "I'm handing in my resignation from this University next year," adds Matthias. "There is altogether too much feminist politics on the one

---

[29] Luigi Reina, "Come ti conto un fatto: *Due vocazioni* di Rimanelli" in *Su/per Rimanelli: Studi e Testimonianze* (*Misure Critiche*: Salerno) XVII-XVIII (Oct.-Dec. 1987, Jan'June 1988): 153.

[30] Giose Rimanelli, *Due vocazione* in *Il tempo nascosto tra le righe* (Isernia: Marinelli, 1986).

hand, and altogether too much worldly-minded activity, on the other." (73)

Ironically, within the anaconda species, the females are considerably longer than the male. They could, therefore, exert greater pressure over their male counterparts, because of their physical length, and be able to control their surroundings better than the male. The female anaconda could squash the male with very little effort and, thereby control the species and the environment in which they reside. Freedman suggests that it is the female populace of the university atmosphere, those women who are not producing as much as their male counterparts nor receiving positive reviews, that is strangling his professional existence, like the boa, and for that reason, he is renouncing his position within the, now, secular world of academia.

As a child, Matthias Freedman attended the Nuremburg trials of 1945-46. His grandparents were killed by the Nazis at Dachau, so he focused his attention on the Nazi ringleaders. In the post-war period, the Nazi prisoners, in an attempt to exculpate their horrific actions of the war years, utilized political and social word games as the validation for their savagery, relying on linguistic game plan patterns to alter and revise the history of an era. Thirty years later, now in the contemporary period, Freedman finds himself in a similar situation in which political language is, once again, transforming the present academic reality. However, from his perspective the power hungry, right wing political position that is now willing to kill in the name of socio political reform appears to be the female faculty on the university campus.

The theme of governmental abuse within the university atmosphere reverberates in Rimanelli's earlier English novel, *Accademia*, and although it is also present in this new text, it plays a different, yet still decisive role in *The Three-Legged One*. It serves as an allegorical component depicting the power struggles within the confines of this restricted universe. In this narrative, the University hierarchy functions, with all its political machinations and semantic word games for self justification, as the metaphor for the Nixon Administration: self-righteous and quasi dictatorial. It is, therefore, the actual politics of the day, the immoral deceitful politics of Washington, D. C. and the Watergate debacle, which attest to the false reality that has now entered the sacred world of the American democratic system.

The voyage between chronological and fantastic time occurs, one evening, in which several of the colleagues and friends of Vera and Simon congregate to watch their new documentary, *The Twelfth Macaque*. Simon and his colleague, Andrew, determined to fashion a film based on some of the prevailing sexual theories of the day without, either one of them taking a personal stance on the subject. The purpose of the film was to entertain and elicit reactions from their coworkers at the university. However, a debate ensued and reactions were divided between genders.

The horrific past that Simon experienced during the war years in Italy, begins to reappear this evening in the responses the film generates. The film elicits a multiplicity of interpretations ranging from gender roles and choices, to gossip mongering in the university, to religious heresies. One male colleague, Anacleto Zinghelli, saw the theme of betrayal and the story of Judas, while a female colleague, Charlotte Shark, saw the film as a "comic operetta on hedonism" (47). Their dichotomous political perspectives sets the stage for the imminent political battle and it is through this maze of symbols and signs that Simon will need to navigate in order to survive. Politics, although not present from Simon's point of view in his film, has taken the center stage in this present period of his life and it manifests itself within the power struggle of the male/ female relationship.

Simon points out, the evening of the film, that:

> I'm perfectly alone: yet memory continues to make something of the past surface to consciousness, and offers me the continuity of time. (37)

This idea runs parallel to that of Mircea Eliade's of cosmic time. According to Eliade, the religious man in general lives in a recurrent present. He repeats the signs of another and, through this reiteration, lives always in an atemporal present.[31] History is, as Vico proclaims, cyclical in nature, and in the case of Simon, his Orphic journey is about to repeat itself for the third time.[32]

Ironically, Simon who has never taken a political stance in his life, now was in the middle of a political nightmare. As a youth, he avoided choosing a religious faith so as to not side with one parent or another; during the civil war in Italy, he again avoided taking sides, although he ended up fighting for the wrong side. Now, with his marriage in trouble, friends and colleagues are taking positions. It has become a battle between men and women. Politics and socio-economics have entered into his daily routine. Simon had remained neutral in all the political melees that have circulated around him within his personal and professional radius.

The political nature of family is, furthermore, evinced in Simon's reference to Leon Battista Alberti's book *Della famiglia*. According to Simon, the book bases its substructure on the perception of *virtù*; the ability to control your own fortune. Family, like anything

---

[31] Mircea Eliade, *The Myth of the Eternal Return*, translated from the French by Willard R. Trask (Princeton: Princeton University Press, 1974) 86.

[32] "Nevertheless death pays me a visit every fifteen years, punctually. At age twenty came the resurrection after death in the war. At age 35 my resurrection in America, after death in my native Selimo. And now, on the threshold of fifty, the new shattering blow that draws near. I am so conscious of witnessing myself dying it inebriates me with a new life" (29).

and everything else, therefore, has a political nature. Yet, the contemporary woman sees her life differently than the woman of the Renaissance. Whereas the women in Simon's life are primarily academics and scholars, Alberti's *Della famiglia* stresses that the care of young children is women's work (for nurses or for the mother) thereby relegating the female to a subservient role. The women in Simon's social sphere see male supremacy everywhere. They believe that men are holding them back professionally because of their new political station in life. Simon has supported these women in their quest for equality within the university. But the gender war is not allowing for any neutrality and Simon is their latest target.

A group of women calling themselves the *Regime* have taken a political stance against their male counterparts. The party is lead by Charlotte Shark, a name that arouses all the wildness and ferocity of the ocean by depicting a creature that is dangerous and deadly to man. Most importantly, however, is the physical and psychological description that Carmen Cara attributes to her:

> Charlotte had a nice appearance, but she eternally dressed as a male and wore half-length boots. She was athletic, her laughter was frank, her speech proper, and she gave the impression of having been a voracious reader. The truth of the matter, however, was that she was power-mad and vindictive to the point of hysteria. (46)

The physical appearance is one that brings to mind the Nazi Storm Troopers with their black leather boots and athletic framed bodies. At the same time, her emotional description parallels that of the authoritarian power hungry fascist of the first half of the twentieth century when hate and bigotry controlled the politics of the day.

Simon's career as a scientist began, from his perspective, from a religious basis. Although he never formally chose a religion to follow, his mother was a Catholic and his father was Jewish, Simon believes that he was protected during the Italian Civil War by Eloi. According to Judaism, Eloi, Elijah, is the prophet that announces the coming of the Messiah and, therefore, peace on earth on earth will reign. Christianity, on the other hand, sees Eloi as G-d.[33] The *New Testament*, additionally, claims that Elijah, Elia, is, in fact, John, the Baptist and/or Jesus.

The internal journey of the war years proved, in the post-war years, to lead the young Simon, again from his view point with the help of Eloi, along another path that would take him all around the world in which his scientific studies of physical anthropology become internationally acknowledged. In addition, the reference to Eloi in this new text by Rimanelli, evokes the inaugural narrative of the writer, *Tiro al piccione*. His protagonist, Marco Laudato, is saved and shielded from the barbarism of the war by Sargent Elia. Elia, Elijah, the prophet and the guardian of Marco. The physical and spiritual protection of Sargent Elia throughout the horrific campaigns of the new Republic of Salò are what provide for the protagonist to return safely to his family home and start his life anew.[34]

The sanctity of the workplace now eradicated, Simon, instead, attempts to re-create it within the confines of his own home with Vera. Again, the house, which should serve as his *axis mundi,* as it has in all of Rimanelli's previous writings, instead now operates as profane space and will, ultimately, be the location from which this marriage will fail. There is no sanctity within any of the abodes in which Simon and Vera live. Their first house, in New Canaan, Connecticut, was a gift from his mother-in-law, Dress. She, ultimately, evicted Simon from the home with the birth of his son, Daniel, out

---

[33] And at the ninth hour Jesus cried with a loud voice, saying, Eloi, Eloi, lama sabachthani? Which is, being interpreted, "My G-d, my G-d, why hast thou forsaken me?" (*Mark* 15:34).

[34] "'Sì, ma,' allora dissi, e adesso sapevo che era necessario tornare in mezzo alla gente, vestito con i miei panni civili, e vivere finalmente per una ragione" (263).

of rage and jealousy. The second home is in Vancouver, Canada. Vera refers to this city as Vaffancu. As they are setting up that house, an earthquake shakes the city, rattles the walls, and destroys many objects in their home. Finally, in Anaconda, Simon attempts to realize, once again, a sacred space: his own residence with Vera. His house serves as a meeting place for friends, family and students. In this residence, people come to study, eat celebrate and have sex. Within this locale, Simon, in addition, tries to remake his own personal *axis mundi*, the center of their personal/sexual sacred space: the small bedroom.[35] However, although Simon would like the room to be his personal temple, it has, become, as Vera asserts, the place from which he does his vendettas;[36] the sanctity of their love has been desecrated by their extramarital relationships and their pseudo incestuous pairing.

Vera refers, on several occasions, to Simon as "Daddy", and "Father;" and Simon acknowledges that Vera is more like a daughter than a wife.[37] Both recognize that their relationship is of an incestuous nature and, because of this, it is doomed to fail, as each has become aware in the course of these entries. This idea runs congruent

---

[35] "I make my way to the kitchen, dancing. I grab a basket of red tomatoes and carry it in the small room. Then I go out to the garden and gather some red roses, and I also take them into the room. Finally, I go upstairs to my study and I take down an acrylic painting which I myself made of her: a sweet face with an enigmatic smile, covered by enormous sunglasses. Her amulet, two fish darting in opposite directions, hang from her neck. They are reflected in her sunglasses now transformed into two enormous male members, one in a state of erection, the other in decline. I also bring the painting into the little room, and I arrange a macabre mini-altar on the chest of drawers. I go into the kitchen once more and return with two candlesticks which I light in front of the painting.
"Are you crazy?"
"I've prepared the altar." (25)

[36] "You also brought Evelyn here," she says. "And it is also here that you brought Roseanne. It's always here that you carry out your vendettas" (26).

[37] "You've married your daughter, raping her in the park, offering her candy and making her see your member" (34).

with René Girard's who asserts that sex is an impure act. According to Girard, sexual activity is always accompanied by violence. Moreover, as soon as one violates the boundaries of marriage to engage in illicit relationships (incest and adultery), the vehemence, and the impurity ensuing from this ferocity, grows more authoritative and severe.[38]

The imagery, moreover, that Simon uses with regard to sexual activity with Vera also, according to Girard, refers to impurity. In a sexual encounter that the couple have during their love making in Vancouver, during the earthquake that damaged their home, Vera, unexpectedly, started her menstrual cycle one week early. Menstruation, according to Girard, is also an adulterated act. Women who menstruate are often, in some cultures, segregated from the community. Blood attributed to anything other than sacrifice is considered unchaste (Girard, 33-34). Ironically, in describing the altar that Simon has built for Vera in the small room of their home in Anaconda, he describes the "red tomatoes" and "red roses" that he has placed at the altar, that image of blood primeval in details, is analogous to an unholy sacrifice.

The absence of responsibility becomes a focal point in Vera's journals. She believes that Simon has been untrue in his commitment to her. Yet, he has always been honest in telling her everything. Although their marriage is not traditional nor is it open, they have instituted a truth pact between them.[39] Yet, despite the fact that

---

[38] René Girard, *Violence and The Sacred*, translated by Patrick Gregory (Baltimore: The John Hopkins University Press, 1989) 34-35.
[39] "[...] her mind runs back to episodes of the past, to things that we have done individually and which subsequently we recounted to each other because we had established a truth pat between us. This is our only freedom. It serves us as seductive stimulus to lofty ideals, as a weapon of aggressiveness in both our public and private deficiencies, as a basis for deductive conclusions, and as a warming, coddling baby blanket" (20).

Vera claims Simon is not honest, in fact, it is she who has been dishonest. Her name, Vera, in Italian stands for truth, yet, through the course of her journal the reader learns that she has manipulated truth to fit her situation. At the start of their relationship she tells Simon that she is a virgin, yet through her entries, it is apparent that she has had sexual experiences since she was a teenager. While Simon was married to his first wife, Billie, believing that he would return to her and end their relationship, she feigned suicide. Truth, for Vera, is interpretative and, more importantly, built on lies:

> The most beautiful lies are to be found in the *Our Father* (56 words), in the *Gettysburg Address* (266 words), in the *Ten Commandments* (297 words), in the *Declaration of Independence* (297 words), and in a *Federal Ordinance* (26,911 words) that establishes the price of cabbages for the year. (127)

Vera fails to see that each of these documents is an implied agreement between two sociopolitical groups, although the link between them may be fragile due to interpretation, misuse and abuse, its basic principle is to unite rather than to separate. Yet, misinterpretation and manipulation of each of these tenets has been the reason for civil hostilities in the country and has led to bloodshed. Vera, moreover, adds that "we create these lies for ourselves in order to preserve our attachment to the illusion of permanence" (163). Vera's flawed conviction is to not recognize that these doctrines did not cause the civil unrest in the country, but served to unify and merge the public into a cohesive force. The battles fought came as a result of neglect and perversion to the above principles. They were not falsehoods, but rather truisms that were mutilated in the name of self righteousness. The concept, therefore, of brother against brother, civil war, permeates this text when an administration refuses to accept these beliefs and prefers to misrepresent them in order to lie, cheat and deceive the very people that they are sworn to protect.

The abuse of power, simultaneously, caused by civil authorities provokes in the reader an equally appalling moment in American history that is alluded to within the narration: the 1891 New Orleans Lynching of Italians in the Crescent City. The evening in which Simon and his friends are viewing his documentary, one of the people present is Barth Bellicapelli, a noted authority on the Mafia. Referring to the historical event of the executions in New Orleans of thirteen Italian immigrants, the lector is immediately reminded of Rimanelli's novel, *Una posizione sociale*.[40] In that tale the author drew parallels between nineteenth-century America and Italy of the 1930s. Both countries were divided politically, socially and economically along geographic and racial lines. However, in Rimanelli's novel the author points an accusatory finger to the mishandling of the trial by Joseph A. Shakespeare, the mayor of the city. His mismanagement permitted the masses to kill in the "false" name of justice. Government corruption, the desire to blame an innocent for an event that did not occur to cover-up another wrongdoing lead to the civil melee in New Orleans.

Vera's notion that untruths are accepted to retain permanence is at the heart of the matter with regard to the Watergate scandal. The Administration preferred to lie and cover-up its nefarious behavior rather than confront the truth. The American populace, at the time, was divided into two basic groups: those who wanted to believe that the government could do no wrong thereby allowing the delusive eternalness of a stale and outdated political dogma; and those who wanted the Administration to pay a high price for their deception

---

[40] Giose Rimanelli, *Una posizione sociale* (Firenze: Vallechi, 1959). This novel was re-issued as *La stanza grande* (Cava di Tirreni: Avagliano Editore, 1996).

which would, ultimately, bring about a change that would expand, at all levels, the use of the term democracy.

A parallel anecdote of civil unrest that does not follow the laws established between man and a higher authority does exist within *The Three-Legged One*. At the very start of the narrative, Simon annotates that his eldest son, Sandro, from his first marriage with his Roman wife, Billie, had an inbred animosity towards his youngest son, Daniel, from his second marriage with Vera.[41] The hatred that Sandro directs towards Daniel reminds the reader of the story of Cain and Abel. Sandro is so jealous of his half-brother that only death would appease him. Cain's reaction to his brother was of a political nature: the social politics of the family. Cain killed Abel and when questioned denied any responsibility and knowledge of the act.[42] Cain's punishment was that the fields he tilled would no longer produce, and that he would be a wanderer the rest of his life (*Genesis* 4:12), moving yet further from the periphery of Eden, the paradise from which his parents had already been banished. The blood of Abel was, therefore, absorbed into the earth and it is this very soil that would reject the farmer Cain.

This transgression is not the first in the Old Testament, although it is the first in which the word sin is used (*Genesis* 4: 7). Adam and

---

[41] "[...] This so called brother is actually a stranger as was Sandro for that matter, whose acquaintance he had made only last summer. Nor has Daniel forgotten Sandro, his father's eldest son, a youngster savage and malign, a sly provocateur, who sported a scornful mustache in the manner of a West Point cadet.

In Sandro's eyes Daniel, 'the kid,' was a fat pinkish pigling to be roasted on a spit, to Vera's horror, because through him she intuits Billie's revenge, Billie the Roman lady whose man she had walked off with wantonly and capriciously, subsequently dubbing divorce love.

Nor does Daniel forget the day he fell in the canal on Cape Cod, experiencing the first real terror of his life as drowning in the water, under the eyes of this guffawing stranger who watched him from the bridge." (3)

[42] "And the LORD said onto Cain, where is Abel, thy brother? And he said, I know not: am I my brother's keeper?" *Genesis* 4:9.

Eve ate from the prohibitive Tree of Good and Evil because of pride. Cain, because of envy, kills his brother. Each believes that they are above the laws established by G-d. The sin of Cain is, therefore, the continuation of the one committed by Adam and Eve.

Sandro did not assassinate his brother. However, he did not attempt to save him when he fell into the water and was about to drown; he just stood, watched and laughed. He, as Cain, believed that he was not his "brother's keeper." The extinction of Daniel would remove any barrier between him and his father and it would place him in a position of greater importance. From Sandro's perspective, the death of Daniel would eradicate the marriage of Simon and Vera and provide for Simon to return to his former life and family in Italy. Sandro sees Daniel as his nemesis.

Simon's relationship with Vera had nothing to do with his Roman children and his new life in America. Sandro, therefore, has created a partition in Simon's world: Italy and the United States; his Roman children and his American child, thereby laying the groundwork for an erroneous impediment between two nonexistent distinct worlds. Simon does not recognize a variance between these two spheres; they, his children, are all equal in his eyes, and from his perspective, only one universe exits, and the politics of the family is missing and a fantasy nurtured in the mind of the young man. Sandro's behavior, therefore like Cain's, would only cause contempt in the eyes of his father.

Ironically, at the end of the novel Cara informs the reader that Sandro has, unintentionally, followed in his father's steps and moved to the United States in order to continue his studies in Europe-America politics and economics. Although Simon did not recognize a division between his two worlds, Italy and America, Sandro, who, first, personally fashioned a division between these two entities, is now, professionally, blending together this joint research area without any artificially self imposed boundaries.

René Girard explains that physical violence, in some cases, can be an hallowed act. He states; "violence is the heart and soul of the sacred" (Girard, 31). Girard points out that killing without sacrifice is the fundamental inviolable act because it is the reincarnation of the Cain and Abel's story. The holiness rests in that the sacrificial victim is forgotten and replaced by a surrogate victim (Girard, 5). Abel, the shepherd, had an offering to give to G-d; Cain, the farmer, did not. Cain executed his brother in anger (*Genesis* 4:1-9). Therefore, if, as Girard points out, savagery were a hallowed act, then war, civil war, would be an action that transports man back *illo tempore*.

The author's intimate account of his unwilling participation in Italy's Civil War is not restricted to his first book, *Tiro al piccione*. It is an appalling tale that goes beyond this archetypal narration and is echoed in many of the Rimanelli's stories including *Graffiti, Il tempo nascosto tra le righe*[43] (in which Marco Laudato, the protagonist of *Tiro al piccione*), re-appears in the contemporary era, *Familia, Il viaggio*,[44] *Benedetta in Guysterland, Accademia,* and now *The Three-Legged One*. Each of these narratives, the Italian and the American, carries the reader back and forth between two very disunited epochs (the contemporary period in America and the war years in Europe), but all are bound by a common link in which each country suffered internal civil hostilities. The human suffering and degradation that war entails is wholly brought to light in each of these texts and the social and political turmoil of a nation during various periods of social and civil unrest attests to itself within the narrative frame.

---

[43] Giose Rimanelli, *Il tempo nascosto tra le righe* (Isernia: Marinelli editore, 1986).

[44] Giose Rimanelli, *Il viaggio* (Isernia: Iannone, 2003).

A subtle intertextual element surfaces within the narrative to highlight the incessant civil hostility that Simon witnesses during this precarious period in American society and it revolves around the difficult relationship that exists between him and his mother-in-law, Dress, a wealthy and controlling woman. The name of this woman, Dress, calls to mind, at least to this reader, the German city of Dresden, fire bombed towards the end of World War II. In describing his son Daniel, Simon states that he "fancies himself a member of the master race, like his mother" (3). Dresden, through the centuries, has always been an important garrison as well as a center of military industry in Germany. At the same time, in describing their sexual relationship, Vera, in an entry that pre-dates this narrative (September 24, 1972), states that during lovemaking, Simon's member resembles "the hard metal cap of a German soldier - the bringer of death..." (23).

This idea of the racial superiority of Vera's family reminds the reader of the German position to enslave the world. They were bloodthirsty and in their quest for power and control, did everything possible to betray mankind. A parallel idea, also, occurs in Ferdinando Camon's narrative, *The Fifth Estate*. In that novel, the narrator explains the cyclical nature of history:

> [...] and on this basis the old people could tell us that the Germans were such and so and that in time we'd find out for ourselves, as though each generation must unfailingly have its own experience with war and the Germans, [...][45]

Vera's mother, Dress, had an extremely belligerent attitude towards Simon. Although married to a French teacher, she had a long

---

[45] Ferdinando Camon, *The Fifth Estate*, translated by John Shepley (Marlboro, VT: The Marlboro Press, 1987) 66. Originally published in Italy as *Il quinto stato* (Milano: Garzanti, 1970).

time sexual relationship with an Italian sailor, who died at the start of World War II, which produced Vera. Dress sees in Simon the reincarnation of the lover she lost and does everything possible to break their marital relationship so that she could have a physical involvement with him. She is willing to betray her daughter, without consideration of the dreadful consequences, for a possible union with Simon.

The deadly and direful aim of the Germans during World War II was to conquer the world and declare themselves the Master Race. It was this attitude of superiority that allowed them, from their perspective, to create the "final solution" and attempt to extinguish the Jewish population from the world. This specific atrocity comes to the foreground in the narrative with an episode that tells of the extermination of the grandparents of Matthias Freedman in Dachau. The grandparents, in a letter to their American daughter-in-law, state: "that the life of cockroaches was better than that of prisoners in the hands of the Nazi's" (14).

Dress, the conservative industrialist, believed, in a similar manner, that if she could not have Simon, the independent liberal intellectual, then he must be destroyed and she would do anything to end the relationship between him and her daughter, including bestowing on her daughter a financial settlement to end her marriage to a man she sees as unsuitable or even having him arrested for an offense he did not commit.

At the same time, Vera, in an attempt to manage her relationship with Simon, gave their recently born child Daniel, to her mother to raise. The transfer of the child, from the natural parent to a surrogate evokes the biblical passages of Moses and the story of Exodus in the *Old Testament*. The Pharaoh of Egypt had sentenced all sons of the Hebrews to be killed Yocheved, the mother of Moses, desperate to extend his life, floats him in a basket down the

Nile. Pharaoh's daughter, hearing the cries of the baby, shows compassion for the child and adopts him as her own (*Exodus* 2: 1-10). In a barbed manner, a variation of the same story is presented within this text. Dress has threatened and harassed Simon throughout his relationship with Vera, but never the son. Vera, in order to free herself of all obligations involving this child and to extend her control over Simon, surrenders him willingly, and against Simon's will, to be raised by her mother. Yocheved thought only of the safety of her child and was, as a result, totally altruistic in her behavior; Vera, on the contrary, only thought of herself, and as such, attests to her selfish behavior.

Moreover, Simon, like the Israelites escaping the wrath of the Egyptians, moves across the continent to find a better life, only to encounter that Vera sacrifices their child to a "false" mother. Ironically, Vera deposited Daniel with her mother in the town of New Canaan, Connecticut, a place that should be the parallel of the biblical promised land of "milk and honey" assured to the Jews fleeing captivity. New Canaan, in Simon's saga, is a location that certifies the thrall Vera's mother has over her and produces an isomeric image of the real Promised Land. Simon's journey, therefore, into the "real" Canaan, like the Israelites, will be postponed because of Vera's idolatrous actions; she refuses to abandon the intimate bondage she has towards her mother. Simon, a name that corresponds to one of the twelve tribes of Israel, Simeon, is still in search of a homeland. Throughout his fourteen-year marriage to Vera, Simon moved, professionally, around the country at the bequest of his wife who became bored in each new locale. Each displacement destined Simon to restart his career in a different place. This constant relocation made it impossible for Simon to have a specific dwelling and he was, like the wandering Jew, always seeking a last place to call home. However, this tribe of Israel, like one of the ten lost tribes, finds itself now irretrievable within the political quagmire of a socio historical community. Additionally, the name Simon could suggest a derivation of the Hebrew word Sh'mah, the central tenet of Judaism. It is with these six words that the Jewish people, who recite it four times a day, announce their belief in a monotheistic message in which there is only one G-d. These few words separate the Jewish people from the idolaters who worship false and multiple gods. Vera, who appears to worship a false god in the figure of her overbearing mother, is condemned not to enter the "real" promised land of Canaan and consequently is dispatched only as far as the limits of the pseudo/false New Canaan. Simon, on the other hand, will have to, ultimately, make the journey by himself.

In Simon's journal he describes his child/ wife as "a daughter of the waves like Venus, thin-lipped and with a deep pubis" (77). These words are echoed in Rimanelli's earlier narrative, *Accademia* (73) and in his mini memoir, *Molise Molise*.[46] In *Molise Molise* the author paints a portrait of his ex-wife as a "figlia dell'acqua come Venere," a romanticized image of the female based on the famed Renaissance painting of Sandro Botticelli. Botticelli's representation is one of three, and as such, a type of trilogy, much like the authors' English language books. The first of the paintings is known as the *Birth of Venus*, the second, *Primavera* and the last, *Pallus and the Centaur,* all painted during the penultimate decade of the fifteenth century. Each of these three classic paintings play a role within his narrative, however it is the third that plays the most significant function in this third part of Rimanelli's trilogy.

The last work of art is *Pallus and the Centaur* and was not discovered until 1975, the year in which this novel was originally composed. The composition of the painting, like this narrative, focuses

---

[46] Giose Rimanelli, *Molise Molise* (Isernia: Libreria Editrice Marinelli, 1979) 151.

on two figures: a centaur, a lusty half horse, half human, and a guard nymph armed with a shield. The woman has been identified as both the goddess Pallas Athena and Camilla, the chaste heroine of Virgil's *Aeneid*. The artistic work deals with the triumphant struggle of virtue over sensuality through the use of reason. The two parts of the human soul are represented, on this canvas, by the double nature of the centaur.

However, in *The Three-Legged One* the chastity of the female is nonexistent, although the male counterpart views their life together as a "journey of sex." (3) Vera has informed us of her various sexual escapades, initiating when she was an adolescent of fourteen. Although she has been married to Simon, coincidently, for fourteen years, she dreams of being sexually involved with other men, and even her dreams betray her as she acts them out within the fantasy. Contrary to the virtuous Camilla, Vera is corrupt in her behavior, sexually and ethically; she has one set of rules for Simon and another for herself. Virtue does not triumph in this novel as it does in the Botticelli canvas, but leads the two characters down a path that will take them to the bowels of earth.

Yet, *Primavera*, the second in the Botticelli trilogy, is according to *La vita nuova*, the name that Dante gives to Giovanna, a friend of Beatrice, who, consequently, foretells only the coming and not the arrival, of his *donna angelicata*.[47] Rimanelli possibly recognizes that his relationship with the second wife is not an ideal intimate connec-

---

[47] According to the Florentine, she is called *Primavera* because: "Quella prima è nominata Primavera solo per questa venuta d'oggi; ché io mossi lo imponitore del nome a chiamarla così Primavera, cioè prima verrà lo die che Beatrice si mosterrà dopo la imaginazione del suo fedele. E se anche vogli considerare lo primo nome suo, tanto è quanto dire 'prima verrà', però che lo suo nome Giovanna è da quello Giovanni lo quale precedette la verace luce, dicendo: *Ego vox clamantis in deserto: parate viam Domini*" (See, Dante Alighieri, *Vita nuova. Rime*, a cura di Fredi Chiappelli [Milano: Mursia, 1965] 55.

tion, but rather hints, as Dante does at the end of *La vita nuova*, that there is still much more to come.[48] At the same time, as Rimanelli suggests his failed personal rapport with his second wife in *Molise Molise*, Simon, in *The Three-Legged One* also acknowledges the same unfavorable realization. The emergence, therefore, of this Giovanna in Rimanelli's text, who is not the ideal female he had hoped, suggests that Simon (as, too, the author) has not found his *donna angelicata* and that another, unseen as yet, will appear.

Moreover, within this narrative there is a specific reference to Dante when Vera remembers a poem Simon had written for her entitled *New Life*. Simon's poem should evoke in the reader Dante's book *La vita nuova*. Paget Toynbee explains that *La vita nuova* is the first autobiographical work of modern literature.[49] It gives the account of the uncontaminated adoration that Dante has for Beatrice and the memory of an ideal love for his *donna angelicata*.

In a paradoxical style, the story of Simon and Vera is an extreme variation of the love story between Dante and Beatrice. Vera is not portrayed as the *donna angelicata*, but rather the woman who has forced this scientist into another hell by comparing her to Eve in the Garden already in cahoots with the serpent.[50] Simon and Vera do not portray ideal lovers, rather their relationship is built on only sex, and sex for them "is another life at the portals of death" (4).

Dante, alone, composed the *Vita Nuova*. The reader does not get to perceive any of Beatrice's direct reactions yet, it is known that

---

[48] "Sì che, se piacere sarà di colui a cui tutte le cose vivono, che la mia vita duri per alquanti anni, io spero di dicer di lei quello che mai non fue detto d'alcuna" (Vita nuova, 76).

[49] Paget Toynbee, *Dante Alighieri: His Life and Works*, edited by Charles S. Singleton (New York: Harper & Row, 1965) 160.

[50] "With their pact, with their embrace, and with the resultant pleasure they have expelled him from the Terrestrial Paradise. They have forced him to descend into the pits of hell, like Orpheus, to look for his Euridice-Innocence, Euridice-Capacity to love" (43).

they never had a physical linkage. In contrast, *The Three-Legged One* presents two different journals, written by two distinct persons: the first, from Simon; the second, from Vera, and even commented upon by a third party, Carmen Cara. They both discuss the disintegration of their fourteen-year relationship by centering in on their sexual activity. Dante did not have an actual tangible association with Beatrice. However, whereas Dante's *little book of memory* is dedicated to his adored lady who had just died, the narrative of Simon and Vera is one that deals with the death of a relationship and is dedicated, according to Carmen Cara, to the reader so as to glean "some teachings of an edifying character" (xix).

The transition between the present and past continues to penetrate the text when, in his journal, Simon states that "memory makes me hallucinate" (2). This state of fantastical visions creates, ultimately, the instrument that transports Simon, and the reader, *illo tempore*. He becomes a type of shaman who through his visions transports the reader to the start, *ab initio*, of creation.

Eliade adds that the initiation rite of the neophyte shaman often implies a crisis so deep that it appears to border on madness. The fledgling priest must resolve the catastrophe in order to become the anticipated sage of his community. It is a mystical initiation; an inaugural sickness that exacerbates the symbolism of initiatory death. This scientist also points out that the first sickness follows very closely the classic ritual of initiation: a basic change in an existential condition; the novice emerges from his ordeal endowed with a totally different being from that which he possessed before the initiation; he has become another.[51]

The shamanic vocation is not profane. It produces a traditional mystical pattern. It is a symbolic return to the precosmogonic Chaos

---

[51] Mircea Eliade, *Rites and Symbols of Initiation: The Mysteries of Birth and Rebirth*, translated by Willard R. Trask (New York Harper Torchbooks, 1958) x.

that precedes any cosmogony. Eliade, further, states that this return is equivalent to preparing a new Creation. The psychic chaos of the new shaman is a sign that profane man is being dissolved and a new personality being prepared for birth (Eliade, 1959, 89). It is the shaman who will climb the necessary ladder leading to heaven on a celestial journey and it is through the upper openings of the *axis mundi* that allows the shamans to set out on their flights (Eliade, 1959, 53-54).

Simons' personal genesis will take him back to his individual history in Selimo and, ultimately, transport him through a labyrinthine passageway that deposits him in the present. It will take him through the horrific war years and his suffering in Villafranca, to his post-war experiences wandering the world as an anthropologist. It will continue through his difficult marriage to his Roman wife, Billie, and finally, take him through his courtship and present marriage, disembarking him in the disintegration of his relationship with Vera.

To allow the reader to accompany him through this Kaleidoscope like maze of personal consciousness and growth, Rimanelli takes us along on Simon's physical and metaphysical journey through the unknown. The author's compositions are, as G. B. Faralli asserts, *un continuo viaggio orfico.*[52] Rimanelli, the writer, functions, therefore, as a type of Virgil, gently guiding us along a labyrinthine path that he hopes will take the reader to higher dimension of understanding of the human experience.

The infernal voyage for the protagonist commences at the start of the narration when Simon, referring to his sex life with Vera, states that it is another life:

---

[52] G. B. Faralli, "*Kakky: Modelli narrativi e linguistici dell'ultimo Rimanelli,*" *Misure Critiche* 17-18 (1988): 216.

Although sex is the most unreal of fantasies, it gives one joy and repose, it is another life at the portals of death. Our sex life, however, is poisoned by social monsters, by boredom, by porno-fantasy and by lukewarm blood. Vera knows this, but she always demands more, and now. She is projected towards regions unknown, and all that is left for me is to await the new unknown. It will be a shattering event, but even that will pass. I hear the blow arriving from the rotten shrubs of our town, Anaconda, New York. It would be possible already to make a souvenir photo of it lightly over-exposed with a black and white 135mm. (4)

This passage prompts the reader to remember Dante's entrance into *Inferno* when the poet, awakening from his sleep, finds himself looking upward to the light and the path that would, eventually, taken him out of the ravine of hell and lead him to the elevation of paradise (*Inferno* I: 1-18).

The presence of Dante and his journey in the works of Rimanelli is not without precedence,[53] and here in *The Three-Legged One*, it is exceptionally clear within the specificity of the text. The precise reference to Dante appears, in an episode in which Simon discusses with his student/lover Roseanne the significance of the number three. It is one of the twenty references that he gives, and ("Terza Rima - See Dante" [72]) the explicit indication, is the nineteenth. Dante commences his journey through the underworld when he reaches mid life, *nel mezzo del cammin di nostra vita*, a time, that according to Allen Mandlebaum, corresponds to the age of 35.[54] Although Simon is forty-nine years old at the time of his journal, he met Vera when he was thirty-five and already suffering from his own

---

[53] Sheryl Lynn Postman, *Crossing the Acheron: A Study of Nine Novels by Giose Rimanelli* (New York: Legas, 2000) passim.
[54] *The Divine Comedy of Dante Alighieri*, a Verse Translation by Allen Mandelbaum (Toronto, New York, London, Sydney, Auckland: Bantam Books, 1981) 344.

personal hell due to his failed marriage with his first wife. His sex life with his second spouse is one that he describes as "a wild journey" and it is this allusion to a dantean type voyage that begins to pierce the darkness within this narration.

Rimanelli, in his novel *Graffitti*, takes the classic Italian tradition of the *stilnovisti* and their view of *la donna angelicata* and inverts the figure to portray her counterpoint *la donna diabolica* in order to present a sardonic, biting view at contemporary society and the emerging and blossoming role women should play in it. The author, again, tackles the function of women in his novel, *Accademia*, by showing them as misusing their new-found power in an academic community.

Vera, in *The Three-Legged One* is not Simon's *donna angelicata* but rather, as in *Graffiti*, his *donna diabolica*. She takes him to the Acheronte with the purpose of leaving him in that deplorable place. Dante describes this zone as the land of the envious.[55] Vera is a casualty of her own arrogance. She is not scholastically equal to her husband and, although she recognizes that she is envious of him, her plan is to obliterate him professionally:

> [...] I was becoming your enemy. Even if I had not gone to see her personally, Anna would have attended to this matter on her own and Susie, in turn, would have informed Charlotte, and Charlotte, Matthias. Soon the State Street feminists would be embracing a new sister and a divorce to boot. Everything suddenly took shape in my mind: the future. Matthias' position was a fragile one. Charlotte probably knew of my old relationship with him and at this point, Charlotte would have blackmailed him. To your harm. I know Matthias. He always makes others pay the toll. And now it would be your turn. Revenge would be mine. (132)

---

[55] "Questi non hanno speranza di morte, / e la lor cieca vita è tanto bassa, / che 'nvidïosi son d'ogne altra sorte" (*Inferno* III: 46-48).

She, mistakenly, has intermingled their personal relationship with his professional career. In her fits of jealousy, she turned to the female academicians within the College with the hope of demolishing his life history.

In a morphological parallel with the work of the Florentine, Rimanelli's variation on the Orphic journey of his protagonist appears in a memory sequence that takes place in chapter 9 when his entire life comes to the foreground:

> Everything takes another course, we slip into the groove. And to register the fall signifies to descend into the Avernus, among the Furies. But one adjusted even to this state of affairs. (78)

The description of Simon's plunge into an inferno like reality within the academic community is strongly reminiscent of Dante's descent and is comparable within the nuances of the narrative. The evening in which he and his friends gather to watch the film the *Twelfth Macaque*, Simon describes the ambiance in the house as; "The smoke had had a hallucinatory effect on all our minds, but the effect seemed also to be boredom" (53). It is at this point in which Simon, searching for Vera, goes down the stairway and finds her in a compromising position with two other people. The imagery of Simon's entry into the dark underworld of sexual politics evokes in the reader Dante's descent into the last circle of hell in which he encounters the betrayers.[56] Here, disloyalty is the sin that carries man to the profundity of Inferno.

Simon's film tells the allegorical story of treachery. He perceives that Vera will deceive him with his friend and counterpart, G. O.

---

[56] "Non era camminata di palagio / là 'v' eravam, ma natural burella / ch'avea mal suolo e di dume disagio" (*Inferno* XXXIV: 97-99).

Shait. Vera's disloyalty will be worse than anything Simon ever did because it has a double aim: the demise of their union, and, she will misrepresent Simon to the female constituency of his academic world with the hopes of destroying his career. Vera uses their personal problems to create havoc in his professional sphere. This personal/professional chaos will, ultimately, take him on his journey into the void of an academic hell in which faculty take political positions based on their gender.

Coincidently, Carmen Cara notes that Simon, although having a deep resentment towards Shait prior to his involvement with Vera, wrote an article about this man's art that he defines as a type of erotic hyper-realism. Among the creative traits that Simon mentions is the art of the cover-up, perceivable within his creations. Shait's artistic ruse, according to Simon's article, allows for the suggestion and the denial of sexual activity at the same time. The ploy suggested by the work of Shait, a cover-up that hints and refutes the actual reality of the moment, allows the reader to see a parallel situation with the Nixon Administration and the Watergate scandal. Nixon betrayed the American populace with dirty tricks and questionable tactics that, ultimately, plunged the nation into a political and chaotic maelstrom that lasted for years. Manipulating and playing with language and truth, the inner circle of the Administration deceived the public. Moreover, once the dishonesty became open, prosecution of the guilty parties, basically, followed political affiliations. The treachery of the governmental process endured within the psyche of the American people for years, even after the resignation of the President and the tribunals of his associates.

Dante and the medieval tradition, the number three is of great importance and consequence. Christopher Ryan, in his essay *The Theology of Dante*, explains the solemnity of the number:

> For Dante, the striving of the human being both to come to individual perfection in knowledge and love, and to reach the perfection in and through a community, *has* its source in the already perfect life of the Trinity.[57]

Structurally, *The Three-Legged One* is a novel in three parts with, three different narrators: Simon, Vera, and Carmen Cara. Each of these voices, moreover, speaks using three distinct voices: there is the "I" for the personal intimacy accorded the diaries; there is the "you" when the journal entries are directed to a specific person; and there is the "he/she" when the narrator of each segment speaks about the other. Simon gives information that he has experienced death on three separate occasions: the Italian Civil War; the end of his first marriage to Billie prompting his departure from Italy to come to America and start his academic career; and now, the end of his personal relationship with Vera that he identifies will come shortly. Each of these death experiences takes place, according to Simon's calculations, every fifteen years. These frightening blazes in his personal life were set in motion when he was twenty and have been unbroken in their consistency to the present time, a span of thirty years; he is now moving into the third cycle of his fifteen year emotional death watch. Professionally, Simon is also having demanding times with three women: Judy Madison, the ex-wife of his best friend and faculty member at the college who wants to have a sexual non-involved relationship with Simon and/or Vera and knows too much about their lives; Charlotte Shark, the Administrator and head of the *Regime*, who wants to see Simon thrown out of the College and plans to use his extramarital affair as the basis for his expulsion; and, Vera, who believes herself to be an academician, although not

---

[57] Christopher Ryan, "The Theology of Dante," in *The Cambridge Companion to Dante*, edited by Rachel Jacoff (Cambridge: Cambridge University Press, 1993) 151.

finished with her studies, at an equal par as her husband. At the same time, there are three females who are creating mayhem in his private life: Dress, his mother-in-law; Roseanne, the female student with whom Simon had an affair; and Vera, his wife who believes that if Simon could betray her, she, also, has the right to do it. Simon's mother-in-law has been in three personal associations: two with Italian sailors and the third, her husband with whom she has minimal contact; Roseanne becomes the third component in a marital triangle; and Vera envisions a *ménage à trois* with Roseanne as the third participant. The importance of the number continues in Simon's own personal history in Europe: he is the first of three children; and the father of three sons. Simon's oldest son, Sandro, is born three years after the publication of his first book (1953). In describing Vera, Simon states that she has never truly been a wife, but rather one of three types of entities: a daughter; a piece of luggage to carry around and open at will; or a semi adult who is writing her thesis. In addition, prior to arriving at Anaconda University, Simon taught at three other institutes of higher education: Yale; British Colombia; and UCLA. The vehicular drive between Anaconda, New York and New Canaan, Connecticut, is an outing that takes three hours. Simon's journal, which originates on August 21, 1974, concludes three days later before the start of the new academic year.

Simon's journal entries end in 1974. However, according to Cara's introduction of this novel, Simon disappeared from sight on May 7, 1976, sending to his friend a copy of the book *Zen and the Art of Motorcycle Maintenance*, suggesting that he has taken leave of the academic world with his motorcycle. Nearly two years have passed since Simon and Vera entered their personal hell. The use of a motorcycle as a means of transport is evocative of Dante's crossing the Acheronte on a journey that would not only lead him out of Inferno, but would also lead him to a new understanding of himself.

Simon, apparently, is making his trek of self-awareness on a motorcycle that takes him away from the bellicose world of the University. The use of the motorcycle in this novel is reminiscent of Rimanelli's earlier book *Molise Molise*. The writer, in that saga, incorporates the traditional epic voyage transposing it to the modern era, and takes himself on a metaphysical journey that, ultimately, shows him all the stages of violence: physical, emotional, political, economic and social.[58]

If we accept that Simon of the 1970s is the resurrected Giose of the 1990s then we can adopt the premise that Simon has, indeed, crossed the Acheronte. He has exited from the political Inferno he endured at Anaconda University and found himself in the present time in Pennsylvania. Daniel, however, is in a new Inferno of another political reality: the AIDS virus and the ability to get the proper medication and its necessary governmental acceptance. He informs the writer that there are new medications, but licensing is not yet granted. At the end of the conversation with Daniel, after having said farewell, Giose writes:

> And we said good-bye with raised hands in the fog, just like two people on the opposite banks of the river. And somehow I was now at peace with myself. (192)

Although Anaconda University is behind him, he now, apparently, finds himself, once again, in a situation in which the government has taken control of another person's life by playing political games. The era has changed; the manipulation of administrative power, however, still, remains. Simon/Giose has traveled through the various levels of Inferno to a new stage of self-awareness. His discussion

---

[58] Sheryl Lynn Postman, "2 + 2 x 2 / 2 = 3: Medieval Hieroglyphics in Giose Rimanelli's *Molise Molise*," *Cuadernos de literatura inglesa y norteamericana*) 7.1-2 (Mayo-Noviembre 2004): 89.

with Daniel suggests that he, too, must, now, endure the voyage to be able to come out on the other side.

Giose Rimanelli's recently released novel, *The Three-Legged One*, appears to be the simple story of marital betrayal. However, duplicity goes far beyond the simple boundaries of marriage. The tale transcends the limits of a traditional restricted narrative and enters into the universal realm of an historical present. The reader, with this novel, witnesses political maneuvering for self justification in committing dishonorable activities. The author has taken the sheltered world of the academic community and transformed its ivy covered facade into an allegorical statement on the internal politics of a corrupt political machine of a specific decade: the 1970s and the Watergate scandal. John Freccero submits that:

> Dante's journey is neither a poetic fiction nor an historical account; it is exemplary and allegorical. It was meant to be both autobiographical and emblematic, a synthesis of the particular circumstances of an individual's life with paradigms of salvation history drawn from the Bible.[59]

In a similar manner, Rimanelli's tale makes use of autobiographical elements to create a fictional universe in which his character, Simon, must navigate in order to free himself from the swamp of falsehoods he encounters in his life to be able to journey on a solid path that leads him to the grandness of truth. Colbert I. Nepaulsingh, in an essay he wrote regarding this narrative in an earlier version, states that the name Simon comes from the Hebrew and means *he who listens* and *he who believes*.[60] Rimanelli believes, wholeheartedly, in

---

[59] John Freccero, "Introduction to *Inferno*," in *The Cambridge Companion to Dante*, edited by Rachel Jacoff (Cambridge: Cambridge University Press, 1993) 179.

[60] Colbert I. Nepaulsingh, "'Rimanelli nelle rime': Life and Fiction, Life and Death," in *Su/Per Rimanelli, Misure Critiche* (1989): 233.

the American form of government. He believes in the democracy that it entails. However, recognizing that there are problems within the system means that the listener, the believer, does not relinquish his desire to find the truth. Truth, according to Rimanelli's novel, is a journey that transports the other to another time and reality so as to see the present in its proper context. He concludes his novel with two simple words: *Veritatis splendor*, truth radiates and, accordingly, humanity wins.

INDEX

Alberti, Leon Battista, 124,125
Alighieri, Dante, 2, 3, 18, 34, 35, 37-44, 49, 88-95, 138-140, 142-147, 149
Auerbach, Erich, 49

Barolini, Teolinda, 43
Bigi, Brunella, 28
Boccaccio, Giovanni, 3, 13, 18, 43, 63, 65, 77, 78, 95, 111
Bonaffini, Luigi, 24, 27, 68, 73, 117
Botticelli, Sandro, 87, 137, 138
Bush, George W. President, 30

Calvino, Italo, 11,12, 45, 62
Camon, Ferdinando, 134
Capek-Habckovic, Romana, 15-17, 26, 45, 48, 63, 64
Cecchetti, Giovanni, 58, 59, 114

Demme, Johnathon 107

Eliade, Mircea, 22, 30-33, 66, 69, 76, 80-82, 86, 103, 104, 119, 124, 140, 141

Faralli, G. B., 141
Fontanella, Luigi, 16
Ford, Gerald, 115, 116
Freccero, John, 149

Gardaphé, Fred, 28,29
Girard, Rene, 30, 75, 76, 128, 133

Gusdorf, George, 57, 113

Harrison, Robert Pogue, 91

Lennon, John, 26
Lejeune, Philippe, 57, 113

Mueller, Roseanna, 57
Mussolini, Benito, 2, 37, 113

Najemy, John M., 49
Nepaulsingh, Colbert I., 149
Nietzsche, Friedrich, 29
Nixon, Richard M., 2, 3, 99, 105, 115, 116, 123, 145

Petrarca, Francesco, 18, 95
Porta, Antonio, 114
Postman, Sheryl Lynn 100, 148
Propp, Vladimir, 11, 61

Reina, Luigi, 57, 121
Rimanelli, Concettina 67, 116
Rimanelli, Vincenzo 67, 116
Ryan, Christopher, 35, 93, 94, 145, 146

Santana, Carlos 26
Starr, Edwin, 26
Svevo, Italo, 90

Tamburri, Anthony Julian, 13, 29
Taylor, James, 26
Todorov, Tzvetan, 114

Toynbee, Paget, 89, 139

Vasari, Giorgio, 87
Vico, Giambattista, 29, 82, 124
Virgil, 27, 39, 46, 73, 89-92, 138, 141

About the Author

Sheryl Lynn Postman (Ph.D., SUNY Albany) is Professor of Spanish and Italian at the University of Massachusetts, Lowell. Her areas of specialization include the contemporary Spanish novel, the contemporary Italian novel, and Italian-American narrative. She is the author and/or editor of numerous books, which list: *El viaje infernal en Los Diarios de Miguel Delibes*, Libertarias (2010) and *Crossing the Acheron: A Study of Nine Novels by Giose Rimanelli* (2000) among her authored books, and *Greece and Italy: Ancient Roots and New Beginnings.* Co-editor with Mario Aste and Michael Pierson (2005) and *Film and Multiculturalism.* Co-editor and contributor, with J. Helí Hernández (2001), among her edited volumes. Her more recent articles have dealt with the figures of Orazio De Attellis, Giose Rimanelli, and Miguel Delibes. Professor Postman has also received grants from the American Association of Teachers of Italian and the National Endowment for the Humanities for summer seminars on language pedagogy and literary theory and methodologies.

SAGGISTICA

Taking its name from the Italian–which means essays, essay writing, or non fiction–*Saggisitca* is a referred book series dedicated to the study of all topics, individuals, and cultural productions that fall under what we might consider that larger umbrella of all things Italian and Italian/American.

Vito Zagarrio
: *The "Un-Happy Ending": Re-viewing The Cinema of Frank Capra.* 2011. ISBN 978-1-59954-005-4. Volume 1.

Paolo A. Giordano, editor
: *The Hyphenate Writer and The Legacy of Exile.* 2010. ISBN 978-1-59954-007-8. Volume 2.

Dennis Barone
: *America / Trattabili.* 2011. ISBN 978-1-59954-018-4. Volume 3.

Fred L. Gardaphè
: *The Art of Reading Italian Americana.* 2011. ISBN 978-1-59954-019-1. Volume 4.

Anthony Julian Tamburri
: *Re-viewing Italian Americana: Generalities and Specificities on Cinema.* 2011. ISBN 978-1-59954-020-7. Volume 5.

The following volumes are forthcoming:

Luigi Fontanella
: *Migrating Words: Italian Writers in the United States.* ISBN 978-1-59954-041-2. Volume 7.

David Barone and Peter Covino, editors
: *Essays on Italian American Literature and Culture.* ISBN 978-1-59954-035-1. Volume 8.

Peter Carravetta
: *After Identity: Critical Challenges in Italian American Poetics and Culture.* ISBN 978-1-59954-036-8. Volume 9.

www.ingramcontent.com/pod-product-compliance
Lightning Source LLC
Chambersburg PA
CBHW020902090426
42736CB00008B/465